AMERICANS ON THE MOVE

AMERICANS ON THE MOVE

A History of Waterways, Railways, and Highways

WITH MAPS AND ILLUSTRATIONS

FROM THE LIBRARY OF CONGRESS

RUSSELL BOURNE

FULCRUM PUBLISHING

GOLDEN, COLORADO

Published in cooperation with the Library of Congress

Frontispiece:
In a photograph from space,
roads may be seen
as main characters in the
geography of Salt Lake City.

*Dedicated to
M. R. G.*

Travelers prepare to
depart via one transportation
mode or another in an 1882
lithograph entitled "The
World's Railroad Scene."

Copyright © 1995 Fulcrum Publishing

Book design by Stephen Kraft
Cover Image: First locomotive to cross the
Allegheny Mountains. (Courtesy of the Prints and
Photographs Division of the Library of Congress)

Library of Congress
Cataloging-in-Publication Data

Bourne, Russell.
    Americans on the move : the history of waterways,
railways, and highways ; with maps and illustrations
from the Library of Congress / by Russell Bourne.
        p.   cm.
    Includes bibliographical references and index.
    ISBN 1-55591-183-8
    1. Transportation—United States—History.
2. Transporation—Social aspects—United States.
3. Transportation and state—United States—History.
I. Title.
HE 203.B68 1995   94-40626
388'.0973—dc20   CIP

Printed in Korea

0 9 8 7 6 5 4 3 2 1

Fulcrum Publishing
350 Indiana Street, Suite 350
Golden, Colorado 80401-5093
800/992-2908

Contents

Foreword by James H. Billington, The Librarian of Congress   vii

Preface   viii

Acknowledgments   ix

CHAPTER 1:   The Dream of a National Road   2

CHAPTER 2:   John Fitch's Plan for Westward Waterways   36

CHAPTER 3:   Rolling into the Empire of the West   62

CHAPTER 4:   Designing the Mobile Society   90

Afterword   124

Bibliography   128

Sources   130

Index   131

An advertising page from 1879
uses an exciting scene of
arriving and departing trains
to hype products of all sorts.
(next page)

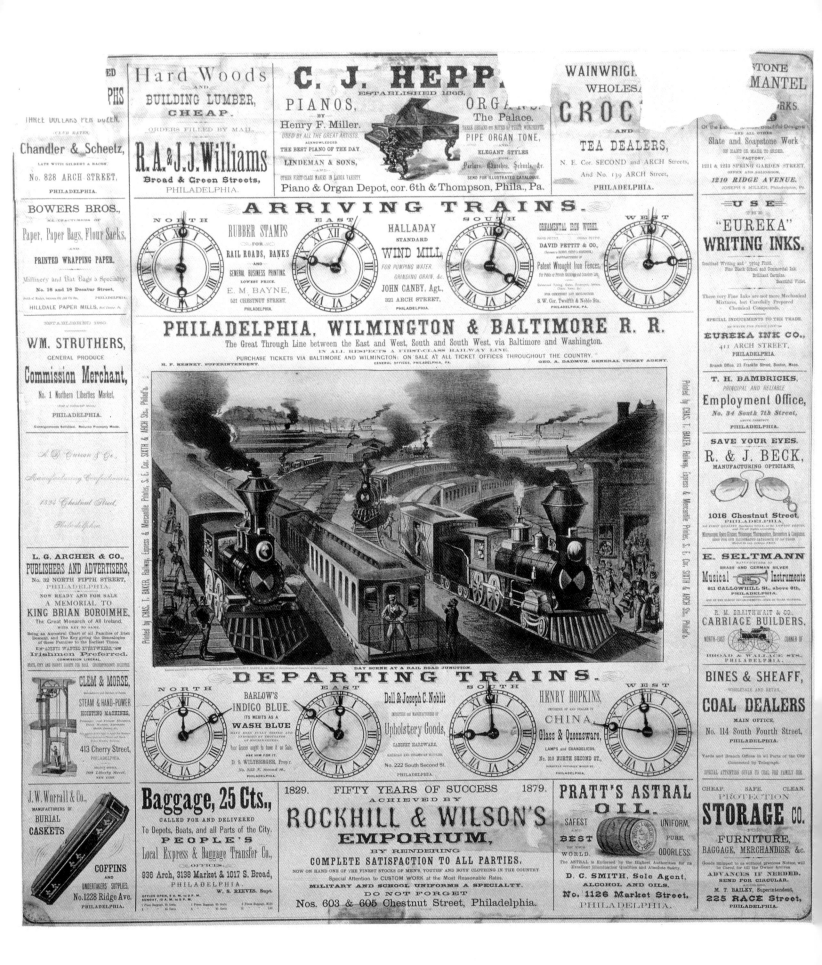

DAY SCENE AT A RAIL ROAD JUNCTION.

Foreword

James H. Billington, The Librarian of Congress

As the oldest national cultural institution in the United States and the largest repository of knowledge in the world, the Library of Congress has the obligation, as well as the joyful task, to open its vast holdings—now more than 104 million items—to all inquiring minds. The free, unhampered pursuit of truth by an informed and involved citizenry was central to the beliefs of Thomas Jefferson, the Library's principal founder. It is also a vital part of the Library's mission today.

Not everyone in need of its resources can visit the Library. Thus, we have many active programs, and others still in planning stages, to bring information on our collections to the broadest possible audience—what I call "getting the champagne out of the bottle." New technologies and informational formats are making the dissemination of knowledge more efficient and thematically diverse, augmenting the perpetually valuable "old technology" of the book.

In keeping with our mission to share the treasures in our own storehouse, the Library is working with Fulcrum Publishing in the publication of a series of books called the "Library of Congress Classics." These volumes offer a general textual overview of a subject which is then fleshed out and enriched by annotated illustrations. All of the material—verbal and visual—is derived from the Library's nonpareil holdings of rare books, periodicals, manuscripts, prints, photographs, motion pictures, recordings, and sheet music—the champagne in our bottle, so to speak.

The books in the "Library of Congress Classics" series are written by seasoned experts in their respective fields who are assisted by the Library's curatorial and publishing staff and resident scholars. *Americans on the Move* is the fifth in this series. The previous four are *The First Americans, Mapping the Civil War, Gentle Conquest: The Botanical Discovery of North America,* and *Prints of the West.* Several more exciting titles in this series are expected in coming years.

Americans on the Move was written by Russell Bourne, a journalist and historian whose insatiable curiosity for telling details of the American experience was, prior to this endeavor, exercised during a long and distinguished career as an author of books on American history and a writer and editor at Time/Life Books, Smithsonian Books, American Heritage, and National Geographic. Mr. Bourne has, in fact, completed another volume in this series, *American Inventors, American Life: 1790–1920,* which will be published at a later date. For his history of American travel and transportation, Mr. Bourne has combed our diverse holdings with an eye for the unique image that will, in conjunction with his informed text, bring this subject to life.

Thomas Jefferson was himself a catalyst for the development of America's transportation system. His boundless curiosity about what lay to the west was an impetus for the Lewis and Clark Expedition, which left its own indelible mark on our national consciousness and sent thousands of Americans on the move over the following two centuries.

Preface

17458—"Why! Good Afternoon! Yes it is a shame, He should have fixed that before we came."

The caption of this end-of-century spoof has the stranded lady saying to the on-coming gent: "Why! Good afternoon! He should have fixed that before you came."

While in the Rare Book and Special Collections Reading Room of the Library of Congress I was reassured that the project I had undertaken was worthwhile by the words of Albert Gallatin. Of the facilitation of American travel he wrote in 1807, "No other single operation, within the power of government, can more effectively tend to strengthen and perpetuate [our national] union."

I paused for a moment, with Gallatin's remarkable essay in hand, to consider more fully my immediate assignment. I had been asked by Fulcrum Publishing (through their Washington representative, Mark Carroll) to write a book on how Americans came to be travelers, based on documents in the Library of Congress. There I was in the Library's inner sanctum, and Gallatin—the man handpicked by Thomas Jefferson to be secretary of the treasury—was graciously supplying me with a clue to the relationship between government and transportation.

This endorsement was tantamount to having the project okay'd by Jefferson himself, the president-statesman-intellectual whose private book collections were to form the basis for the Library of Congress. And that, perhaps, meant that the Library would supply many another clue. The project was, then, not impossibly daunting, even for a writer whose strengths were more journalistic than historic or bibliographic.

Thanks to that double encouragement, I went ahead. I invite you to read the resultant book in the spirit of the institution that fostered it, a spirit of tolerance and generosity.

Russell Bourne
Ithaca, New York

Acknowledgments

When an author is turning away in farewell from such an eminent institution as the Library of Congress, it seems gratuitous to call back over the shoulder, Thanks. But memories of the many kindnesses and courtesies granted by the respective divisions of the LC are so staying—and so pertinent to the way this book developed—that I must try to express them.

The first memory is, however, impertinent. As I was leaving the LC's Manuscript Reading Room after a day's work, I was challenged by a security guard and asked (according to the agreed-upon procedure) to remove my suit coat for a search. The guard noted, after examining the coat and deeming it free of documents, that some of the lining was coming unstitched. "Would you like me to clip off that thread, Sir?" the guard asked. "Otherwise the whole thing may unravel."

Gratefully, I consented. Although that incident had nothing much to do with the quality of *Americans on the Move*, it reminds me of how obliged I am to the myriad behind-the-scenes workers at LC who helped make my visits there effective and secure. In a similar fashion, I extend thanks up along the line—particularly to the workers and chiefs in the Library's Rare Book and Special Collections and Geography and Map Divisions—who assisted me and my wife in our search for illustrations as well as for text nuggets. But because most time was spent in the hospitable aisles of the Prints and Photographs Division, it is to that division that I owe the most heartfelt gratitude.

On both working and executive levels, I wish to recognize the helpfulness of Dana Pratt and Alan Bisbort of the Publishing Office. In different and complementary ways they gave me what keys I needed to enter the research gardens within the LC—as well as a sense of excitement about the process of exploring. But, of course, what mistakes and omissions re-main in this book are my errors alone, much as I would like to lay them at some institutional door.

Beyond the Library of Congress, I thank the many friends and relatives beneath whose roofs my wife and I enjoyed hospitality while conducting researches in Washington. Of that coworker, Dora Flash Bourne—who devoted uncountable hours to picture research and text editing—being with her has been this book's special joy.

Libraries Across the Land

Thanks also are owed to research assistants in many libraries beyond the District of Columbia. Indeed, in the course of writing this book, I was given the awesome feeling that all libraries within my reach are, essentially, substations of the Library of Congress. That feeling was underlined the day I first walked into the vast and multifaceted library facilities of Cornell University (a walk occasioned by the fact that I live nearby). The kind deskperson introducing me to the system looked up to ask, "Are you familiar with the LC system?" Suddenly I wondered whether I was in Ithaca or Washington.

The librarians in this city (both county and university employees) as well as in my sometime hometowns of Litchfield, Connecticut, and Castine, Maine, I thank for their patience and insight. Their cooperation reminded me that this process of public access and free interpretation—the legacy of Thomas Jefferson—is a uniquely American privilege.

AMERICANS ON THE MOVE

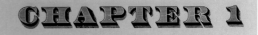

CHAPTER 1

THE DREAM OF A NATIONAL

This pioneer suspension bridge near Niagara Falls was celebrated in an 1856 lithograph.

ROAD

Speaking for his fellow Americans in the last century, Walt Whitman wrote, "Oh public road! You express me better than I can." And in our own century, John Steinbeck wrote of his characters that "the highway was their home and movement their means of expression."

We are indeed people on the move, on the road. The perceptive eighteenth-century commentator J. H. de Crèvecoeur (the essayist who posed that challenging question "What then *is* the American, this new man?") recognized that traveling would be the Americans' destiny: "Americans are the western pilgrims, who are carrying with them that great mass of arts, sciences, vigour, and industry which began long ago in the east; they will finish the great circle."

Walt Whitman, opposite above, sang of the American wanderer; Thomas Jefferson, opposite below, advocated a National Pike. But as late as the 1920s, the travel of many Americans—like those on the Kentucky footbridge, right—was restricted by primitive roads and bridges.

We know and believe some of this; our experience and our faith tell us (rightly or wrongly) that to build another highway is to better our own chances as well as to expand the region's economy. Arthur Schlesinger, in his *Cycles of American History*, advises that because of this cultural quirk Americans are compelled to see life itself as a process of motion. For us, historically, life could never be a matter of static order, as it might have been for Europeans or Asians.

We also believe that this psychological condition is the result of—a kind of gift from—our American continent. Robert Frost, in his unforgettable poem delivered at President Kennedy's inauguration, explained that "the land was ours before we were the land's." The vastness of our continent inevitably conditioned us: we had to cross it by road and rail and river and make it ours; we were blessed or cursed forever with this itch to keep moving, this congenital mobility.

In terms of material constructions, the results of our compulsion to move ourselves as "pilgrims" across the continent have been colossal. Anything on earth that may be glimpsed from outer space is deemed worthy of wonder—the Great Wall of China, the mouth of the Amazon, and so on. By this measure, our land transportation system is also wonderful: The interstate highway system (for many of its fifty thousand miles) is reported by astronauts to be clearly visible. Less easy to see but equally impressive are the 150,000 miles of railway lines, the most extensive system in the world. In the heyday of canals (1830–1850) America could boast the most far-reaching network of waterways.

Americans responded with a wildly inventive, almost manic energy to the urgings of the Founding Fathers and subsequent leaders of the young republic that we build an "American System" (Henry Clay's term) for crossing the Appalachians and claiming the West. South Carolina Senator John C. Calhoun put it this way: "Let us bind the republic together with a perfect system of roads and canals; let us conquer space."

Building that early, nineteenth-century system—which, as will be explained in subsequent chapters, was anything but a seamless process—may also be viewed as the first important step in the industrialization of the United States. Schlesinger and other historians regard our development of land and water transportation routes as the essential "infrastructure" on which all other developments have been based. Transcontinental mobility created a unique production-marketing system—an economic advantage over all other nations or combination of nations. Mobility can, therefore, be viewed as the key to our national wealth as well as to our cultural character.

Reading the Roads of America's Pioneers

The highways and waterways that have been scratched upon the face of this continent in the last three centuries have been called "artifacts of America's civilization." These ways across the land are, nevertheless, difficult to interpret—as inscrutable as most national symbols. Like Egypt's Sphinx and England's Stonehenge, they yield not easily to historic examination.

It's unclear why Americans did respond so enthusiastically to statesmen's urgings that we span the continent. Certainly the people's own desire to get going, to claim their westward heritage, must have had much to do with it. With more affection than amusement, the great British essayist Thomas Carlyle wrote to his friend Ralph Waldo Emerson of this spirit. "How beautiful," he wrote in 1849, "to think of lean tough Yankee settlers, tough as gutta-percha, with most *occult* unsubduable fire in their belly, steering over the Western Mountains to annihilate the jungle, and bring bacon and corn out of it for the Posterity of Adam. There is no myth ... equal to this *fact*."

Carlyle was quite right in describing this as a two-way operation: settlers out toward the West and products back toward the East. Curiously, many historians of the American scene, enraptured by the legendary attractions of the

West, have overlooked the importance of the eastward transport. Yet it was the palpable need of settlers in western New York to export their salt and potash back East that gave financial reality to the dream of the Erie Canal in 1817; it was the similar need of farmer-settlers in Ohio that forced politicians to deliver on the idea of a national road from Wheeling to Baltimore in 1808.

Those economic potentials gave our nation's founders the courage to speak out for improved transportation, the idea of a nation enlivened by internal communications. Henry Clay—who, for his advocacy of greater roads and canals to unify the country, merits praise as patron of U.S. internal improvements—fought tooth and nail during the presidential campaign of 1824 for a greater federal role in the building of turnpikes. His vision (in that small-country era before the Mexican War or the acquisition of California and Oregon) reached out across the continent, across society. He wrote:

5

I shall pay material regard to the interests and wishes of the [newly] populous parts of the State of Ohio, and to a future and convenient connection with the road which is to lead from the Indian boundary near Cincinnati, by Vincennes, to the Mississippi at St. Louis. ... In this way we may accomplish a continuous and advantageous line of communication from the seat of the General Government to St. Louis, passing through several very interesting points, to the Western country.

This does indeed sound like the statesman of sufficient mind and character to command a social revolution against the standpattism of the previous, Federalist administrations. Despite fears that too large a government role in internal improvements might be unconstitutional, Jefferson and his followers continued to support the daring idea of a

Not today, nor tomorrow, but this government is to last, I trust, forever; we may at least hope it will endure until the wave of population, cultivation and intelligence shall have washed the Rocky Mountains and mingled with the Pacific. And may we not also hope that the day will arrive when the improvements and comforts to social life shall spread over the vast area of this continent?

In the preceding generation, President Thomas Jefferson had been among the most eloquent advocates of facilitating westward and eastward passages. His own navigational improvements on Virginia's Rivanna River had enabled his neighbors and other upcountry farmers to get their goods to eastern markets. In 1808 he took on leadership of the move for government construction of the National Pike, or National Road (which, planned to reach the Ohio River at Wheeling, would go on to the Mississippi by crossing Ohio and Indiana). In his compelling announcement of February 19, 1808, he promised:

REPORT

OF THE

COMMISSIONERS,

APPOINTED BY THE PRESIDENT

OF THE

UNITED STATES OF AMERICA,

TO CONFER WITH THE

INSURGENTS

IN THE

WESTERN COUNTIES OF PENNSYLVANIA.

PHILADELPHIA:

PRINTED BY FRANCIS CHILDS AND JOHN SWAINE.

M,DCC,XCIV.

continental nation bound together by arteries of transportation.

For sheer audacity, that concept ranks with Jefferson's vision for another unprecedented institution, the Library of Congress, whose collections were rebuilt on the core of Jefferson's personal library after the British had set afire our national capital and many of its cultural treasures as retribution for the destruction by American forces of Canada's Parliament House in present-day Toronto. And so this statesman, as president and as retired citizen, continued to dream of a nation in communication with itself, from sea to sea, with a vital library at its heart.

Projecting the National Road

Jefferson's championship of the National Road was key to congressional approval of the project's first federal grant. Construction then began in 1808, with little more than human muscle aided by pick and shovel. Nine years of arduous labor later the road (delayed by the War of 1812 but then hastened along as an emergency operation through Maryland, Virginia, and Pennsylvania) finally reached the Ohio border. For its day, it was a super highway. In fact, given the federal source of its funding and the generosity of that funding—Uncle Sam spent $1.75 million to build the mountainous section between Cumberland (Maryland) and Wheeling—the National Road might be seen as proper grandparent of this century's expensive interstate highways.

According to its original design, no grade on the National Road was to be steeper than 4 percent; a thirty-foot-wide roadbed was to be centered on an eighty-foot swath cut through the forests. This was a national, monumental undertaking, and it looked it—rather massive and straight and dull. The roadbed

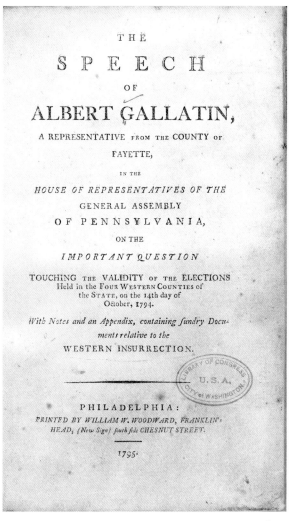

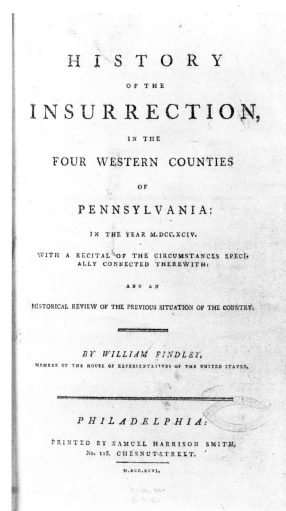

Albert Gallatin, seen opposite above in a portrait by Gilbert Stuart, linked the Pennsylvania rebellion of 1794 to popular anger at poor roads, as enunciated in contemporary papers at left.

North America's earliest
explorers noted the state of
transportation among natives.
Their reports were vividly
rendered in engravings by
German publisher and illustra-
tor de Bry. Viewers of his 1590
Great Voyages can discern
connected towns on Florida's
east coast, opposite; the main
street of a North Carolina
village, right; and a runner, or
"praesfligiator," on a coastal
pathway, above.

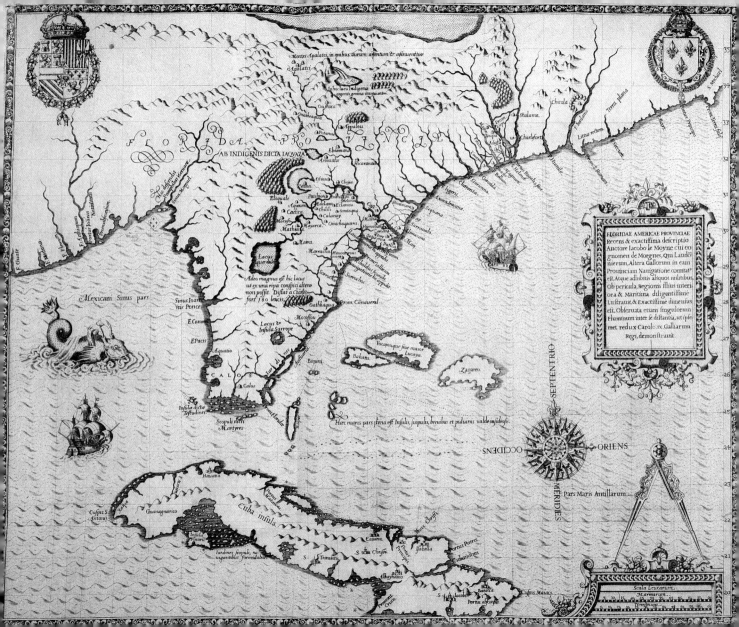

Montes Apalatci, in quibus aurum argentum & æs inueniuntur

Apalatci

In hoc lacu Indigenæ argenti grana inueniunt

Montes Apalatci

Oustaca

Onatheaqua

Apalou

Potanou

Stalame

Chicola

Terra plana

FLORIDA PROVINCIA

AB INDIGENIS DICTA IAQVAZA

Hæc Insula deserta est, quam Incolæ deseruere.

Eloquale

Patchica

Asstma

Cadica

Chilili

Mocoso

Mathiaca

Mayarca

Mawra

Marracou

Chilili

Calanay

Onachaquara

Homoloa

Saravahi

Charlesfort

Hicaranalu

Choya

Hinga...

Garunna

Enacaquan

Amacrana

Mani

Lacus aqua dulcis

Adeo magnus est hic lacus ut ex una ripa conspici altero non possit. Distat a Charles fort 180 leucis.

Sinus Ioannis Ponce

Oathhaqua

Promon: Cañaueral

F. Canou

E. Pacis

Aquatio

Lacus de Insula Sarrope

Mocossou

Mexicani Sinus pars

CALOS

Calos

Insula dicta Tortudines

Scopuli dicti Martyres

Bahama

Yocapouic siue maior Lucaya

Zagareo

Hæc maris pars sterna est Insulis, scopulis, breuibus et puluinis valde insidiosis.

Hauana

Cuba Insula

Cuspis S. Antonii

Guanaguarico

Insula Pinorum

Tardares scopuli, nauigantibus formidabili.

S. Trinitati

Mons Chrsti

Canana

Isabella

Portus Patris

S. Iacobi

Portus absconditus

Cuspis Maици

Pars Maris Antillarum

SEPTENTRIO

OCCIDENS ──── ORIENS

MERIDIES

FLORIDAE AMERICAE PROVINCIAE Recens & exactissima descriptio Auctore Iacobo le Moyne cui co gnomen de Morgnes, Qui Laudo nierum, Altera Gallorum in eam Prouinciam Nauigatione comitat⁹ est. Atque adhibitis aliquot militibus, ob pericula, regionis illius interi ora & Maritima diligentissimè Lustrauit, & Exactissime dimensus est, Obseruata etiam singulorum Fluminum inter se distantia, ut ipse met redux Carolo IX Galliarum Regi, demonstrauit.

Scala Leucarum. Marinarum.

Terrestrium

was made up of crushed stone of varying sizes; when tamped down, the all-weather surface was as firm as the macadamized roads of later years, at least on the Maryland section of the highway. In this section government funds also paid for stately stone bridges (some of which remain in use today as parts of Route 40), impressive enough to elicit favorable comment from European travelers.

At once, the traffic along this first segment of the National Road became, to contemporaries, "almost unbelievable." An astonished Englishman wrote, "We are seldom out of sight, as we travel along on this grand track toward the Ohio, of family groups before and behind us." Summarizing his experience of seeing a nation that had taken to the road, he exclaimed, "Old America seems to be breaking up and moving westward!"

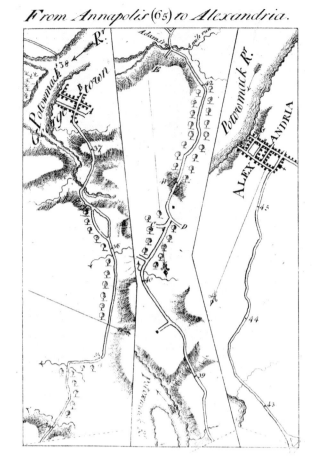

From Annapolis (65) to Alexandria.

Thomas Jefferson's library—the basis of the Library of Congress—contains a copy of New York engineer Christopher Colles's survey of U.S. roads, opposite. Detail from that work, at far right, shows parts of the road from Annapolis to Alexandria. In post-Revolutionary America, such roads were often financed by lottery, below, right.

FROM THE UNITED STATES CHRONICLE.

POST-ROAD LOTTERY.

THE Subscribers, being appointed Managers of a LOTTERY, granted by the Hon. Legislature of the State of Rhode-Island, at February Seſsion, A. D. 1791, for raiſing the Sum of Five Hundred Dollars, in Specie, in Order to repair the South Road, ſo called, leading from Providence in this State, to Voluntown, in Connecticut, preſent the following Scheme to the Public, in which there are leſs than *two Blanks* to *a Prize,* viz.

		Dolls.		Dolls.
1	Prize of	250	is	250
1		100		100
3		50	are	150
4		25		100
10		10		100
31		5		155
77		3		231
1207		2		2414
1334 Prizes.				3500
2666 Blanks.		For the Road,		500
4000				4000

The Objeĉt of this Lottery being to repair the Road uſed by the Stages for tranſporting the public Mail, and accommodating Paſsengers between Hartford and Boſton, thro' Norwich and Providence, the Managers flatter themſelves it will meet with that Patronage and Support, from all Claſses of Citizens, that a Meaſure of ſuch public Utility merits. The Encouragement already given the Managers, notwithſtanding the Multiplicity of Lotteries that prevail at this Time, is ſuch, that they expeĉt to compleat the Buſineſs by the firſt of May next. Notice will be given 'of the Time and Place of Drawing ſaid Lottery, and a Liſt of the fortunate Numbers publiſhed in this Paper.—In the Payment of Prizes the greateſt Punĉtuality will be obſerved by the Managers, who have given Bond for the faithful Diſcharge of their Truſt.—Prizes not demanded within 4 Months after the Drawing ſaid Lottery, will be deemed as generouſly given to repair ſaid Road, and applied accordingly.
☞ TICKETS at One Dollar each, may be had of the Managers, of the Printer of this Paper, and at ſundry other Places, in this and the neighbouring States.
GEORGE WATERMAN,
HARDING HARRIS,   } Managers.
BERNARD MATHEWSON,
Cranſton, March 9th, 1791.

PRINTED BY BENNETT WHEELER.

So he perceived the essential spirit in this get-up-and-go country. And it might appear that, given the apparently fulfillable dream of the National Road, Americans would proceed from one federally financed internal improvement to another, inventing new vehicles, building new bridges, joined in their desire to unite their states and span their distances. It did not, however, happen that way at all; indeed, the fact that the National Road did not reach Columbus, Ohio, until 1833 and Vandalia, Illinois, until 1852 demonstrates that there were problems within the dream, negative forces within the myth of mobility that needed to be addressed. Not only in the case of the National Road, but in the total drama of Americans becoming a mobile society, political backbiting and destructive competition (not to mention technological backwardness and conservative skepticism) were constant companions to the vision and the boldness.

PROPOSALS FOR PUBLISHING

A

SURVEY

OF THE

ROADS

OF THE

United States of America.

By CHRISTOPHER COLLES, of New-York.

CONDITIONS.

1. THAT the work shall be neatly engraved upon copper, each page containing a delineation of near 12 miles of the road upon a scale of about one inch and three quarters to the mile, and parti-

2. That a set of general ————————— upon a small scale with references from ———— to the particular page where the description of any road is to be found ; these maps will then answer as an index and will be found more convenient than any other index that can be made.

3. That each subscriber shall pay one quarter dollar at the time of subscribing (to defray several incidental charges necessary for the work) and one eighth of a dollar upon the delivery of every six pages of the work : but such gentlemen as are willing to advance one dollar will be considered as patrons of the work, and will not be entitled to pay any more till the value thereof is delivered in.

4. That subscribers shall pay 20 cents for each of the general maps and three cents for each sheet of letter press in the alphabetical lists or other necessary explanation of the drafts.

5. That each subscriber shall be considered as engaging to take 100 pages.

6. That non-subscribers shall pay three cents for each page of the work.

These surveys are made from actual mensuration, by a perambulator of a new and convenient construction, invented by said Colles, and very different from any hitherto used, which determines the number of revolutions of the wheel of a carriage to which it is fixed, and is found by experiment to ascertain the distance to a much greater degree of accuracy than could be expected ; the direction of the road is determined by a compass likewise affixed to the surveying carriage.

Account of the Advantages of these Surveys.

A traveller will here find so plain and circumstantial a description of the road, that whilst he has the draft with him it will be impossible for him to miss his way : he will have the satisfaction of knowing the names of many of the persons who reside on the road ; if his horse should want a shoe, or his carriage be broke, he will by the bare inspection of the draft be able to determine whether he must go backward or forward to a blacksmith's shop : Persons who have houses or plantations on the road may in case they want to let, lease, or sell the same, advertise in the public newspapers that the place is marked in such a page of Colles's Survey of the roads ; this will give so particular a description of its situation that no difficulty or doubt will remain about it. If a foreigner arrives in any part of the Continent and is under the necessity to travel by land, he applies to a bookseller, who with the assistance of the index map chooses out the particular pages which are necessary for his direction. It is expected many other entertaining and useful purposes will be discovered when these surveys come into general use.

** Subscription papers will be sent to most of the Booksellers on the continent.

Even Thomas Jefferson had moments of hesitation. Although he had boosted the National Road and had also dreamed of a great road from Washington to New Orleans (via Virginia's Great Valley Road and the Natchez Trace), he quailed when considering the ways and means of achieving desired internal improvements in other parts of the country. President Jefferson had this to say to the New Yorkers who came to him requesting federal funds for the Erie Canal—which, when finally built in 1825 *without* federal help, became the magnificent first link in our system of westward-reaching waterways:

> It is a splendid project ... and may be executed a century hence. Here [in Washington, at the Potomac] is a canal of a few miles, projected by General Washington which has languished for many years because the small sum of $200,000 ... [could not be] obtained. And you talk of making a canal three hundred and fifty miles long through a wilderness! It is little short of madness to think about it.

Certain other American leaders, down through history, have been even more pessimistic than Jefferson about the feasibility of new transportation systems. As late as 1862, when the industrial colossus of the North was engaged in punishing the agricultural South, a high government official was asked if he believed in the dream of a transcontinental railroad. He responded with a snort, "I would not buy a ticket on it for my grandchildren!"

Although the Mexican War of 1845 had inspired visions of coloring the entire continent in red, white, and blue, and although California's gold rush of 1848 had provoked one of the greatest known waves of emigration, the technology for fulfilling the westward dream, whether by a national road or by other means, did not seem to be at hand. Roadways and turnpikes had limitations (led by excessive costs) as did canals. Flimsy railroad lines were no match for the deserts and the Rockies.

Railroads had proved their value only for short hauls between existing termini; few of them made money. In Kentucky, a discouraged railroad operator, disillusioned by the crankiness of steam-powered locomotives, commanded that horses, much more dependable, be put back into harness to haul cars along his rails. In fact, sailing around Cape Horn seemed the only way for desperate emigrants to reach the West Coast. Old-time whaling vessels, pressed into service for the passage, were then left to rot in abandonment at San Francisco's wharves.

Nor was everyone inspired by crossing and opening the land between St. Louis and San Francisco. For example, Senator Thomas Hart Benton, one of our nation's most visionary statesmen, thought the idea of somehow getting across the continent was important only because that would enable us more easily to reach Asia.

The Historic Desire to Stay Put

This mid-nineteenth-century resistance to forward motion, this skepticism about the wonders that could be accomplished through effective transportation, stemmed from a deep-rooted pessimism about the fate of the whole national experiment. The well-recognized author and attorney William Wirt asked rhetorically in 1809, "Can any man who looks upon the state of public virtue in this country ... believe that this confederated republic is to last forever?"

In these negative voices—which spoke out with strengthened conviction after the War of 1812—there was no hint that the act of traveling across the continent might be in any way advantageous. Even Chief Justice John Marshall, solid in his expectations for the American republic and its constitution, agreed with those who saw no point in moving on to the West. He described this historic, stand-pat point of view:

> The country beyond the Cumberland Mountain still appeared (to the dusky view of the generality of people of Virginia) almost as obscure and doubtful as America itself to the people of Europe, before the voyage of Columbus. A country there was—of this none could doubt who thought at all; but whether land or water, mountain or plain, fertility or barrenness, preponderated— whether inhabited by men or beasts, or

both, or neither, they knew not. If inhabited by men, they were supposed to be Indians—for such had always infested the frontiers. And this had been a powerful reason for *not* exploring the region west of the great Mountain, which concealed Kentucky from their sight.

During the colonial years when the ideals of a free democratic society were being formulated in certain sectors, the very idea of gadding about was frowned on. Governor Winthrop of the Massachusetts Bay Colony, upon being given an elegant sedan chair with leather straps and silver buckles (probably the loot from a captured Spanish galleon) for his possible travels, rejected the vehicle summarily. To the approval of his fellow Puritans, he claimed he had "no use for it."

Later, during the Revolution, when Connecticut's Governor Trumbull visited the town of Norwich, he created an uproar by arriving in a dandy little chaise. The sober, hardworking inhabitants of this preindustrial community—whose contact with Hartford and the world of international mercantilism was minimal—were so amazed by the extraordinary vehicle that all work came to a halt.

This dramatic nineteenth century view of Cumberland Gap emphasizes the loftiness of a key passageway through the Appalachians, discovered by Thomas Walker in 1750.

Indeed, this was the era when a heavy farm cart, with four creaking wheels, was regarded as not necessarily a wise investment. Could those wheels do the farmer any good, given the lack of roads? Bumpy and broken-down "corduroy roads" (logs arranged in horizontal rows across the path of a swampy roadway so that passing wheels would not sink into the muck) usually represented the best cross-country roadway that was available. Why risk a good wagon on anything like that? Even in sophisticated Philadelphia of 1761 only thirty-eight wheeled vehicles existed. It was the era of saddle horse and pack train on land, or of pole-boat on rivers.

The American colonies' astonishing lack of all-weather roads and wheeled vehicles was, it might seem today, such a barrier to travel that the very idea would be ruled out entirely. But Americans of that era approached travel somewhat differently, believing that the best way to go was by river or, if you had to take an overland route, by sleigh in winter. At any crossroad community, the winter scene was enlivened by dozens of sleighs and sledges, drab working vehicles or gaily decorated pleasure conveyances, waiting to be whisked off across the landscape. These people could get around; yet the fact is that, for much of the year, most of them did not want to.

It cannot be said that all Americans, all through our history, have been willing to leap upon the next vehicle. Mobility came upon us gradually, as an eventual persuasion of us by continental forces, that this might be our destiny.

Three Roads into the Wilderness

The British authorities who once regarded themselves as masters of North America commanded the colonists to restrict their real estate ambitions to territory within carefully defined limits. Although the 1760 victory over France's globally minded monarchs had ceded most of the continent east of the Mississippi to Great Britain, and although certain ambitious gentry (including George Washington) yearned to saddle up and explore and claim slices of the new lands, royal policy forbade colonists from moving westward. The Proclamation Line

The log-surfaced road opposite, found in Montana, replicates the old, imperfect practice of "corduroying" muddy routes. A well-equipped freighter above recaptures eighteenth century "Conestoga" wagons.

STEAMBOAT LINE.

STAGE NOTICE
FARE REDUCED!

COHASSET, SCITUATE & THE GLADES

On and after Tuesday, June 28th,

A STAGE will leave COHASSET for HINGHAM, connecting with Steamer Nantasket for BOSTON, at 6:30 & 9:45 A. M. and 3:30 P. M. Leave BOSTON at 9 A. M., 2:30 & 6:00 P. M.

FARE THROUGH, FROM COHASSET TO BOSTON, 35 CENTS.

The proprietors of the South Shore House will run a Carriage to meet every Stage to and from Boston.

FARE THROUGH, FROM SCITUATE HARBOR TO BOSTON, 60 CENTS.

GRAY'S CORNER, 55 CENTS.
GANNETT'S " 50 "

Capt. HENRY SYLVESTER will be in readiness with his boat on the arrival of each Stage, to convey passengers to and from the Glades House.

Fare through from BOSTON to the GLADES, 60 Cents.

J. W. RICHARDSON.
JAMES BEAL.

COHASSET, JUNE 28, 1859.

Propeller Job Press 142 Washington St., Boston.

Abraham Bradley's map of 1796, right, tried to chart accurately the Post Road and valid overland routes of the day. Not until the next century could stagecoaches offer inexpensive, punctual service as advertised in the Massachusetts poster above.

17

WATERLOO INN.

the first Stage from Baltimore to Washington.

The earliest coaches on the Post Road—like the one halted at Waterloo Tavern, above—had curved roofs and an egg shape to increase strength. Later vehicles, like those extolled in the *Coachman's Guide*, opposite, were lighter, with flat roofs.

of 1763 was established from Maine to Georgia along the crest of the Appalachians in a deliberate effort to keep the restive colonists in their proper place and to keep the perpetually short-changed native Americans within their "Indian Reserve."

Nonetheless, speculators and adventurers saw rich possibilities in the western lands newly won from the French. North or South, Americans viewed land as their fundamental business. The grand, expectant names Vandalia and Transylvania appeared on various promotional maps beyond the Appalachians. Scouts and hunters such as Dr. Thomas Walker and Daniel Boone found ways to penetrate the

mountainous wilderness and to open these desirable domains west of Virginia and south of the Ohio River. Key to those transmontane lands was the Cumberland Gap, once traversed only by Indians and wildlife, discovered in 1750 by Walker.

That explorer wrote that the Gap "may be seen [from] a considerable distance. On the South side is a plain Indian Road. On the top of the Ridge are Laurel Trees marked with crosses, others Blazed with several Figures on them." The picturesque Gap, positioned where an ancient river had broken through the mountain chain, had a floor pounded firm by the feet of innumerable bison.

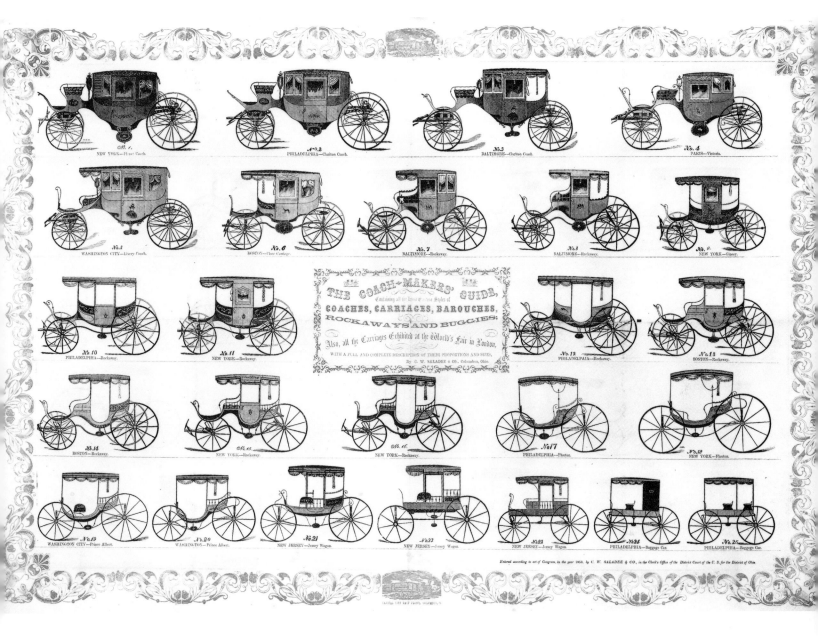

This exceptional topographical break-through allowed Daniel Boone, fur hunter and veteran of the French and Indian Wars (who had been exploring in the area since 1767), to construct his westward-reaching, one hundred-mile-long "Wilderness Road." The road was actually an extension of his preceding, by then well-established, route called "Boone's Trail," which helped adventurous colonists climb from western North Carolina up and over the Proclamation Line into the unknown forests beyond.

Along the Wilderness Road, Boone led a band of fifty settlers (who first had to cope with slashing their way through "turrable cainbrakes") to what would later become Kentucky. The fron-

tier community of Boonesborough was thus established in 1775. Two years earlier, a previous effort by Boone had been defeated by Cherokee Indians who had caught the settler band right in the middle of the narrow Gap. Boone's son was among two who were captured, tortured, and killed.

The Virginians who subsequently followed Daniel Boone through the Cumberland Gap may be characterized as exceptionally, almost fanatically, self-reliant and resolute. An observer wrote with amazement that this dreadful road, "the worst on the continent," cut by washouts and rock slides, was "jammed with immigrants" into Kentucky. Year after year they

19

THE CELEBRATED

THE STUDEBAKER WAGON.

STUDEBAKER WAGON.

struggled up this southernmost of our westward passages, until more than eighty thousand had established themselves as residents of the new territory. Willing for reasons we may not comprehend to trek all those punishing miles on foot or by packhorse, they cannot be seen exactly as models for later, comfort-seeking American travelers. Yet there was something in these independent, colonial Virginians and Carolinians—some special sort of determination to possess one's own land—that found its way into the American character.

By contrast, the travelers of colonial America's northern regions tended *not* to take to the road as individualists. These were not tempestuous younger sons and daughters breaking away from home to seek their own westward domains; instead, they were members of established families who chose to live and behave (and even to move) within a community context. The Puritan Massachusetts and

THE ROAD, — WINTER.

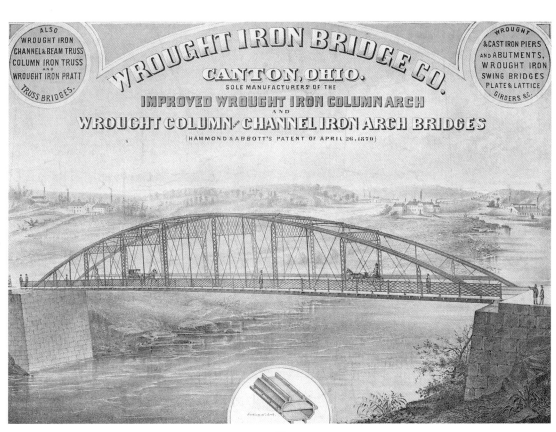

When U.S. roads finally improved in the nineteenth century, so did work and sport vehicles—witness the famous Studebaker wagon above opposite and the sleigh depicted in the Currier & Ives engraving below opposite. Essential to better travel: Better designed and constructed bridges, like those advertised left.

Connecticut families who emigrated westward in the seventeenth and eighteenth centuries did so as parishes or societies—with very little emphasis on individuality. Bringing their altar silver with them, they swarmed out of New England, along the Hudson and Mohawk valleys. The latter route was recognized, even before the Revolution, as the northernmost of the three possible routes through or around the Appalachians; soon after the Revolution, in the enthusiasm for traveling west that then flourished, the Mohawk Valley would become the site of the monumental Erie Canal.

The central of the three routes that led west, dictating the course of American history, was the one up the Potomac River and into western Maryland and Pennsylvania to the Ohio. Historically, this so-called Cumberland Road (for Cumberland, Maryland, not for the Cumberland Gap) was the route that British General Braddock took in his disastrous French and Indian War campaign of 1755. Daniel Boone had the unpleasurable assignment of serving as the general's guide.

With three hundred axmen clearing the way, Braddock built a military road sufficient to transport twenty-five hundred soldiers and hundreds of supply vehicles. Not much earlier in history, this had been the bloody trail to Fort Duquesne (now Pittsburgh) which George Washington had followed with the intention of persuading the French to leave; he lost the argument and barely survived the engagement. Throughout time, Fort Duquesne has been a crossroad location helpful to interior passages; in the mid-1700s, it was simultaneously France's chance to link Canada with Louisiana, and Great Britain's chance to link mid-Atlantic to Midwest.

General Braddock and his huge force suffered even more heavily in 1755 than had Washington and his small band: The general lost his life and nearly a thousand men. His defeat was partially avenged three years later when General John Forbes, accompanied by twelve hundred kilted Highlanders, cut yet another great road through the wilderness of southern Pennsylvania and walloped the French at Fort Duquesne, thereupon renamed Fort Pitt. Braddock's campaign and Boone's

leadership were recalled, at the beginning of the next century when the building of America's prime roadway—the National Road—proceeded along that very route.

Connecting Maryland and Pennsylvania with Virginia and Kentucky in colonial times was a transverse route called the Great Road (taking its name from the Indian trail it followed, the "Great Trading Path"). It ran through the Shenandoah Valley and tied in with the Wilderness Road at the foot of the Cumberland Mountains. Along this ages-old route, additional thousands of northerners streamed westward across the Appalachians in the generation before the Revolution, a migration which, in its totality, has been called "one of the most important events in American History." For it was because Americans had actually settled these transmontane territories that Great Britain could make no claim on them during the peace treaty negotiations of 1782. The lands had become unarguably American, made so not by bewigged statesmen but by foot-slogging homesteaders.

A Revolution in Transportation

In the summer of 1775 the Continental Congress voted to send George Washington forward with all possible speed from Philadelphia to Boston—along with earnest prayers that the newly elected commander-in-chief might somehow relieve the siege of New England's starving capital. Having set out on horseback, Washington needed a full twelve days to complete the trip. When the exhausted, dust-coated general finally arrived at the encampment of the Continental Army at Cambridge, the plodding-in of horse and rider seemed so slow-paced and unremarkable that the sentry failed to record the event in his day book.

Yet with the winning of the Revolution and the emergence of a national American spirit, something nearly miraculous happened. One hundred and fifty years of little progress on the transportation front were swiftly terminated. By 1793, the trip along George Washington's route from Philadelphia to Boston took but five days. One

speedy coach line claimed to have cut the time from Boston to New York to little more than three days. In this era of the young republic, a new generation of would-be travelers demanded speed, swift vehicles with springs beneath their wagons' chassis, and roads that were passable in all seasons.

How to explain this sudden turnaround? How to explain the sudden passion for a national road, for long-distance travel by the clock without delay, time and distance surrendering to the pounding of hooves, the whirring of wheels, the blowings of horns and whistles? By 1860, horses ridden in relays by boys of the Pony Express could cross the entire country in fewer days (ten and a half) than Washington had required to reach Boston from Philadelphia (twelve). These wonders occurred as mere prefaces to the greater accomplishments of the United States in land transportation in the twentieth century. Given our pedestrian beginnings, whence suddenly came this driving spirit?

Furthermore, how did it happen that, in the name of progress or change or advancement, traditional means of existence could be abandoned and mobility become the accepted mode of being for our culture? Did this happen by democratic decision and national policy? If not, who were the travel boosters with sufficient sagacity to foresee the economic consequences, sufficient genius to invent the land and water transportation systems, sufficient talent to banish skepticism (if only temporarily) and sell the concept of buying a ticket and getting aboard?

In his notable Niagara suspension bridge, above, J.A. Roebling demonstrated how wire cables and stiffened trusses could help bridges span unheard-of distances.

John Melish's *Travelers' Directory* of 1825 crudely plotted times and distances from Washington to other "principal places," opposite. Soon thereafter canal boats—like those on the Potomac Aqueduct at Georgetown, right—offered travelers less bumpy passages.

Curiously, one important factor in America's dramatic turn from stuck-in-the-mud localism to nationwide transportation mania, and one clue to the answer for the questions above, was whisky. Whisky, or the moving of it.

Rebellion for Lack of Roads

Among its millions of volumes the Library of Congress contains a handsomely printed version of Albert Gallatin's seminal *Report on Roads and Canals*, dated 1808. In its pages (visible courtesy of the Library's Rare Book and Special Collections Division), Gallatin—President Jefferson's Swiss-born, Pennsylvania-settled secretary of the treasury—sets forth the need for devoting $2 million to the cause of "internal improvements." No contemporary European state had the vision to make such a bold, nation-building proposal. To give added urgency to his proposal, Gallatin argued that the most profoundly threatening episode in the young republic's brief history—the backwoods uprising of 1794 known as the Whisky Rebellion—had occurred because of lack of transportation.

What had happened, in brief, was that the farmers of western Pennsylvania took it on themselves to defy the Alexander Hamilton–controlled federal government in Philadelphia. Hamilton's excise tax of 1791, it seemed to them, was discriminatory, aimed specifically at whisky producers, at them. These Scotch-Irish frontiersmen, many of them veterans of the revolutionary war, had crossed the Alleghenies and established themselves on farms cleared from wilderness. To them Hamilton's tax seemed precisely the kind of oppression that the war had been fought to put down. Should they not now, in righteousness, refuse to pay the tax and rise up against Philadelphia, that new London?

When examined in detail, the complaint of the cash-poor western farmers was not so much a matter of political principle as of production and marketing. Being in the fortunate position of having produced more wheat and corn than their frontier communities needed for themselves, they had sought to export their excess over the hills to the markets of eastern Pennsylvania. Also, having no roads on which to cart their bulky wheat bales, they had determined that kegs of whisky—whisky distilled from the wheat harvest—could be transported much more easily.

In kegs slung on either side of a packhorse, the product was carried over to east-facing river ports in greater and greater quantities.

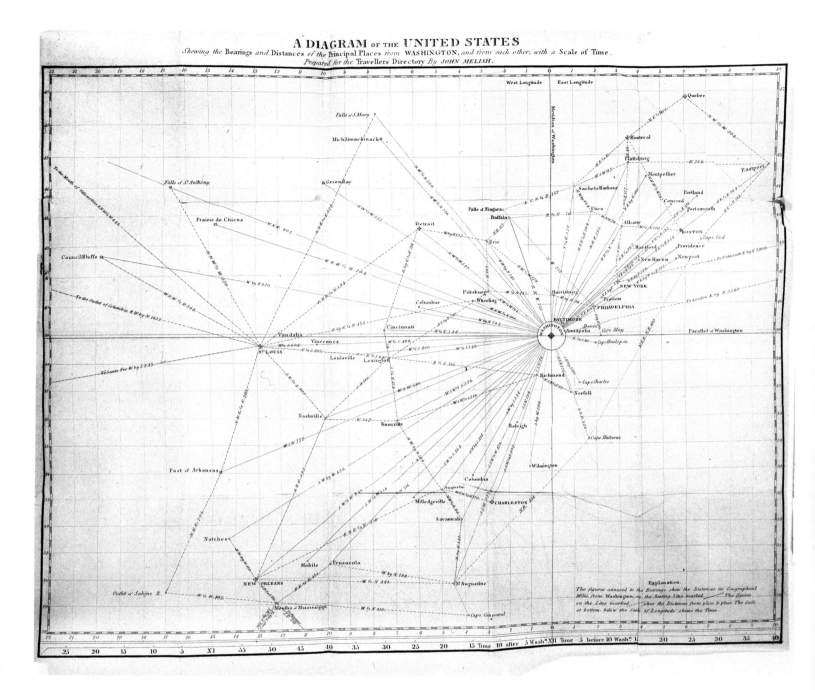

A DIAGRAM OF THE UNITED STATES

Shewing the Bearings and Distances of the Principal Places from WASHINGTON, and from each other, with a Scale of Time.
Prepared for the Travellers Directory By JOHN MELISH.

THE GRAND NATIONAL CARAVAN MOVING EAST.

For American cartoonists in the early 1800s, the road was a great symbol. At right, Andrew Jackson, known as the President from the West, is shown headed east along a turnpike with rag-tag associates and imprisoned Indians. On the way, he might have encountered a toll road sign like the one opposite from eastern New York state.

There, whisky kegs were exchanged for pigs or cattle, with no cash changing hands. So the whisky-producing farmers prospered; and this was precisely the area of wealth that Hamilton had sought to tap with his excise tax. To these farmers it seemed that the federal government was providing no assistance—no roads, no services to aid their communities—and was expecting dollars, many of them, in return. After a number of citizens had been summoned all the costly way to Philadelphia to be fined for nonpayment and to be chastised for disobedience, resentment blazed into resistance.

By midsummer of 1794 western Pennsylvania's angry and well-armed backwoodsmen had taken matters into their own hands, under the fiery leadership of well-educated David Bradford. They attacked a federal marshal who had tried to serve papers on one distiller; they

put to the torch the home of excise inspector John Nevile; they forced armed soldiers, who had been dispatched to stop the violence, to surrender. Tarrings and featherings followed, as well as the rifling of U.S. mail and further destruction of property—indications that government authority had collapsed (just as it had in Shays' Rebellion in Massachusetts, also spawned from an outraged sense of isolation and injustice eight years previously). The government had no choice but to respond with force.

President Washington himself took to the field. Because the sixty-two-year-old patriarch's aching bones discouraged him from riding a horse any great distance, he had to be transported in a phaeton; yet forward he went, calling for the raising of a new army. This demonstration of national determination, along

26

with swift and efficient action by the troops who rallied to Washington's call, dispersed the rebels. A small number of leaders were rounded up and arrested, with two condemned to be hanged. Bradford himself escaped capture; ultimately the troops returned home. Washington subsequently pardoned the convicted rebels.

But the uproar lived on in the minds of many Americans as an example of what might happen to the republic if the backcountry were not united to the coastal cities: the continent would be Balkanized (as we would say today) into a number of hostile nations; all chance of an enlarged, *united* United States would be lost—all because of inadequate transportation for the likes of the Pennsylvania distillers.

Albert Gallatin, representing that rough-and-tumble Pennsylvania territory in the Congress, had been harshly criticized by political opponents for being unable to restrain his constituents. Forever afterward, particularly when serving under Jefferson as secretary of the treasury a decade after the rebellion, he advocated a system of widened, extended, improved roads in order to avoid similar threats to the republic.

Turnpikes and Conestoga Wagons

Pennsylvanians other than Gallatin also got the message. They urged speedy completion of the so-called Lancaster Pike—the sixty-mile turnpike that connected Lancaster (the colonies' largest inland city) and its surrounding, western communities with cosmopolitan Philadelphia. This hard-surfaced turnpike of tightly packed stones upon a base of smaller stones was begun on April 9, 1792, at a time when scientific knowledge of road building in this country was minimal if not nonexistent. The fact that the pike was completed by 1795 (one frantic year after the Whisky Rebellion), at the extraordinarily high cost of $464,142.31, shows that Americans can learn something from history.

Used rather loosely today, the term turnpike originally applied to a road that could not be traveled unless the would-be traveler paid a toll and thus persuaded an attendant to turn aside the pike he used to block the way.

RATES OF TOLL.

	Cents
For a score of Cattle. and in the same proportion for a greater or lesser number,	18
For a score of Hogs or Sheep, - - Ditto,- - - -	5
For a Horse and Rider, a led or driven Horse or Mule. - - - - - - - - - - - - - - -	4
For a Coach, Coachee. Chariot, Phaeton and other four wheel pleasure Carriges. - - - -	18
For a Sulkey, Chair or Chaise and one Horse (2 Cents for every additional Horse)	10
For every Stage-Coach or Stage-Waggon. - -	16
For every Waggon or Cart drawn by two Horses or two Oxen, and one cent for every additional Horse or Ox. - - - - - - - - -	10
For every Sleigh or Sled drawn by two Horses or two Oxen. - Ditto - - - -	4
Every Waggon drawn by one Horse. - - - - -	6
For every other Carriage. - - - - - - -	4

This Board was in use over 100 years, at a gate of the Columbia Turnpike Co. between Great Barrington and the City -of- Hudson N.Y.

Furthermore, in this country, most turnpikes—but not the National Pike of the next generation—were built by individuals or corporations whose objective was simply to derive income from investment in a land-improvement, road-building venture.

Such up-and-coming entrepreneurial efforts were definitely at variance with the Anglo-Saxon tradition, still observed in many states, by which road building was seen as an onerous, regrettable responsibility of a given town. Debtors and other such miscreants within the town might be assigned to carry out the labor in order to "work off" their fines. The predictable result: miserable roads and the discrediting of road building in communities where nobody had much of anywhere to go.

More advanced communities and regions, however, in an effort to direct and improve traffic, would charter corporations (i.e., give them exclusive rights) to build and then to profit from licensed roads. These turnpikes therefore represented an enlightened, eighteenth-century fusion of private interest and public action. The National Pike of 1808

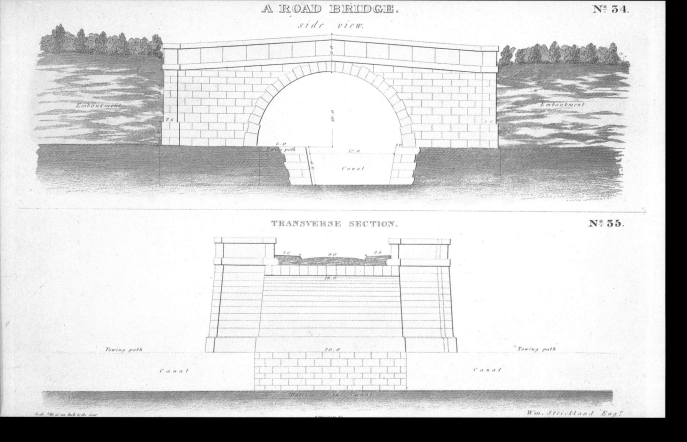

Embankment

Embankment

Towing path

Canal

TRANSVERSE SECTION.

Nº 35.

Towing path

Towing path

Canal

Canal

Bottom of the Canal

Wm. Strickland Engr.

In the pivotal year of 1826, when politicians were deciding which transportation mode might work best, engineer William Strickland delivered the insightful *Report on Canals, Railways, and Other Subjects* to the Pennsylvania Society for the Promotion of Internal Improvements. It included opposite, his exquisite renderings for a double-turning bridge, below, and rails and locomotives, above; and, right and above, for turnpikes and masonry bridges.

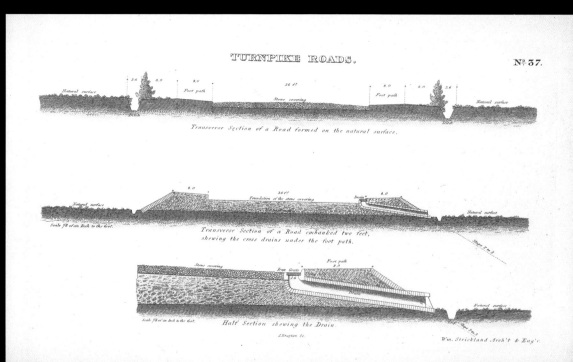

TURNPIKE ROADS.

Nº 37.

Natural surface

Foot path

Stone covering

Foot path

Natural surface

Transverse Section of a Road formed on the natural surface.

Natural surface

Foundation of the stone covering

Drain

Natural surface

Transverse Section of a Road embanked two feet,
shewing the cross drains under the foot path.

Stone covering

Foot path

Iron Grate

Natural surface

Half Section shewing the Drain.

Wm. Strickland Arch't & Eng'r

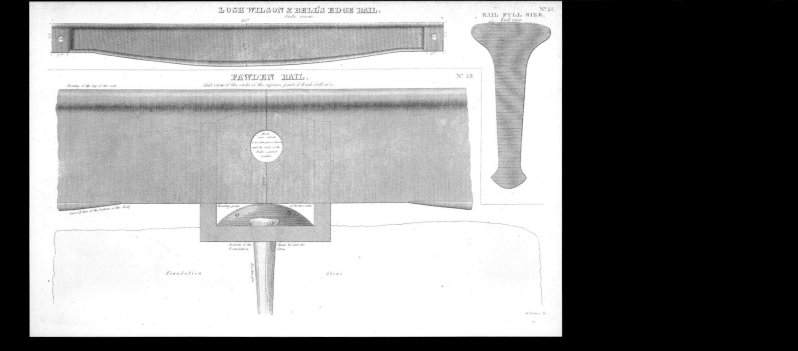

LOSH WILSON & BELL'S EDGE RAIL.
Side view.

N.º 48.

RAIL FULL SIZE.
End view.

FAWDEN RAIL.
Side view of the ends of the square joints of Rail full size.

N.º 49.

Foundation   Stone

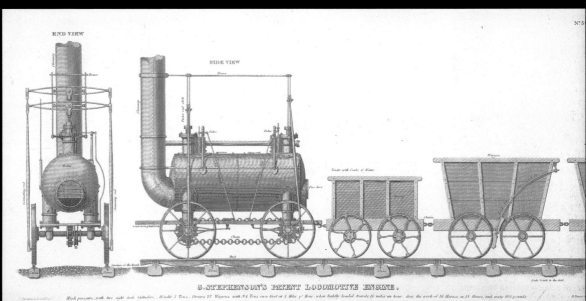

END VIEW

SIDE VIEW

G. STEPHENSON'S PATENT LOCOMOTIVE ENGINE.

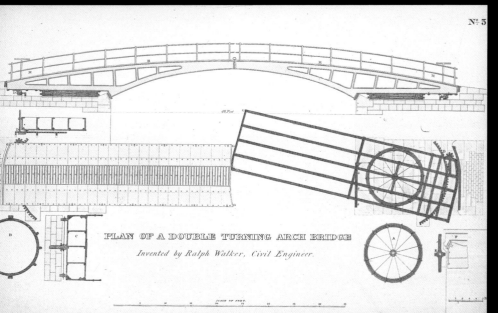

N.º 3

PLAN OF A DOUBLE TURNING ARCH BRIDGE
Invented by Ralph Walker, Civil Engineer.

Wm. Strickland Arch't & Eng'r.

JACKSON TICKE,

Interral Improvement by Rail Roads, Canals, &c.

FOR THE ASSEMBLY
JOHN V. L. McMAHON,
GEORGE H. STEUART.

"Internal Improvements:" a catchy pitch for an 1828 ticket.

would be an even further advancement of the turnpike concept; contracting corporations would be under no risk, accepting funds from the federal treasury, for a road far longer than even the exemplary Lancaster Pike.

In the first year after its completion, an English traveler along the Lancaster Pike had referred to it as a "masterpiece of its kind." By then, the time required for a wagon to rumble from Lancaster to Philadelphia had been reduced from a week to four days. With tollhouses established at 10-mile intervals and traffic rolling heavily east and west in all seasons, the turnpike obviously would earn back its immense initial cost; what had seemed a chancy investment now looked like a gold mine.

There has always been something imperial about major roads. The "King's Highway," "the Royal Road" (El Camino Real), and other such lofty names were given to those grand constructions, which were too expensive for mere citizens to undertake. The cost of the Lancaster Pike—more than $7,500 per mile—was far beyond the capacities of most of the republic's small and hard-pressed communities.

Pennsylvania's fortunate farmers, uniquely blessed with continuing agricultural surpluses and mindful of the "horrors" of the Whisky Rebellion, chose to take the limited risk of building their superior highway (which would remain the best in the country for de-

cades). Additionally, they and other farmers elsewhere had long needed some vehicle to get their hay to market down whatever roads might be available—and to get back from the manufacturing cities the hardware needed for increasingly efficient tools.

Pennsylvania, which would eventually be seen as the "keystone" in the arch of national unity, possessed no sizable coastline along which sail-powered vessels might carry valuable, agricultural freight. In addition to improved roads (and the careful employment of rafts and scows for shipping on the rivers), this state's agricultural communities had a special need for large wagons. Farmers yearned for large, heavy-duty land-ships from which goods would not tumble as they rolled their way over the rough seas of ruts, roots, and boulders.

A distinctive vehicle evolved during the middle decades of the 1700s in the general area of Lancaster. Farmers in the Conestoga River valley (original spelling of the Indian name: *Conestgoe*) had experimented with heavy wagons whose iron-rimmed wheels measured nearly a foot wide and whose carriage beds had a distinctive sway from front to back. The result of this configuration was a wagon that could keep its load aboard even under the bounciest conditions. As handsome as they were utilitarian, the Conestoga wagons' underbodies were most often painted blue, with the upper woodwork a complementary red. Rising gracefully up from the sideboards were seven or eight arcs or bows over which an unbleached but white—always white—cloth could be slung.

Though no speed merchants, the Conestoga wagons—hauled usually by oxen but often by teams of horses—were rugged enough to keep moving under most conditions, without breakdowns or upsets. In the early nineteenth century (after the completion of both the Lancaster Turnpike and the National Road), they made the distance from Wheeling to Baltimore in fifteen days. Eventually, as the roads and ferries of the nation improved, score upon score of Conestoga wagons were seen shuttling between East and West; eventually the traffic was so heavy that a wait of three days was often required at a crossing of the Susquehanna River.

Pennsylvania folklorist Howard Frey heard

tell of a young Moses Hartz of Lancaster County. That ambitious lad went from penniless youth to successful teamster, farmer, and minister on the strength of his abilities with a Conestoga wagon in the early 1800s. It was not just that young Hartz handled the six-horse team well or succeeded in ranging far into Ohio on various hauling projects; it was that he became, like Yankee skippers across the seas, a traveling merchant. Exchanging the farm produce of the wagon's owner for other goods, and always increasing the exchange, he arrived home with a load of clover seed that was sold at a tremendous profit.

The age of uniting the continent by exchanges across its spaces was dawning. Moses Hartz was a truly mobile American, created by his land and his time, as well as by his own personality.

"The road seemed actually lined with 'Conestoga' wagons, each drawn by six stalwart horses, and ladened with farm produce," wrote a traveler along the Lancaster Pike in 1826. Dependable, enduring, the Conestoga wagon eventually became a symbol of American competence in cross-country freight handling; once perfected, like the whaleboat, there never seemed any need to change the form in all its hundred years and more of service to the nation.

Flying Coaches and On-time Stage Boats

Inspired perhaps by the success of the Lancaster Pike and its swarming vehicles (as well as by canal construction and other technological progress during the pivotal period before and after the Revolution), many Americans developed a yen to roll—as fast as possible. No longer satisfied with river-breasting pole-boats and Daniel Boone's packhorses, these impatient citizens of the young republic called not only for comfortable coaches but even for schedules that would be kept night and day.

The postal service which Benjamin Franklin had established for the United States in the earliest years of the Revolution was partially responsible for this accelerated pace. Speeding the mail between the coastal cities without delay was seen as an urgent national duty—if only because that was good for business. The postal service was at that time under the Treasury Department, with mail delivery viewed as a money-making operation. The Post Road that ran from Maine to Florida, with "Franklin stones" marking the miles, was the chief artery of this system; by 1790 there were 1,875 miles of exceptionally well-maintained post routes, along which private and commercial vehicles could fly to their destinations.

The arrival of the stagecoach at a typical location was a triumphant—also self-consciously nationalistic—moment. Painted on the panels of the brightly colored coaches were portraits of famous Americans—Franklin prominent among them. Although the early vehicles had been egg-shaped in profile (perhaps so that lengthwise timbers could compress and bear the strains without cracking), the tops of the coaches gradually became flatter, heavier, and stronger.

This design change occurred as more and more Americans took to the road, with more and more luggage; the flatter roofs could hold the load. The firm of Pease and Sykes (which, in 1785, had won the first contract to carry U.S. mail) also made the business more efficient by replacing the rough-and-tumble "captains" of yore with professional "conductors" who were able to see to fare collection as well as to driving.

Along with better roads and coaches during this post-Revolutionary period went a remarkable improvement in bridges. Enoch Hale's timber truss bridge across the broad Connecticut River at Bellows Falls, Vermont (1785), was regarded as evidence that American road-builders had graduated to a new level of engineering sophistication. Equally impressive was a bridge called the "Colossus" across the Schuylkill River upstream from Philadelphia—a span of 340 feet, built in 1812. The world's first scientific analysis of bridge trusses was written by Squire Whipple, published in 1847, the same decade in which William Howe secured his richly productive patents for wooden truss bridges. Gradually, by a mixture of native skill and applied science, Americans were taking a rational (and businesslike) approach to the process of internal improvements.

THE TELEGRAPHIC CANDIDATES.

Sold By TURNER & FISHER, N.Y. & PHILAD:

CASS.   BUTLER.   CLAY.   TAYLOR.   FILLMORE.   ABOLITION.   M. VAN BUREN.

Cartoonists continued to categorize candidates by choices of travel systems: Opposite, incumbent President Van Buren's blindered wagon horse slips on (Henry) Clay, while Harrison's hard-cider locomotive roars past; above, Zachary Taylor rides a train of "no principles," while other candidates approach the White House via odd conveyances, including telegraph wire.

Where no bridges existed, coaches continued to rely on ferries and river-craft, a mode of traveling that had changed little since the birth of Christ. The coach line charged its passengers no fees for these water segments of the total journey. When longer water voyages were necessary—across Chesapeake or Narragansett Bay—and when a sailing vessel had to be employed to supply that linkage, the line advertised itself as offering "stage boat" service. Whether the water passage was short or long, however, the passengers were consistently assured that there would be excellent taverns available upon landing, fit for "victualling" (from which word came "vittles") or for spending the night.

These taverns of the late eighteenth century were an essential—though not necessarily enjoyable—part of the traveling experience.

Neither men nor women expected to have rooms to themselves. Often, when the upstairs rooms for lodgers were full, passengers would be obliged to bed down with nothing more than their overcoats on the floor of the main room downstairs—as near to the fire as possible. The teamsters and coachmen had to take the lowest accommodations, often in the unheated stable.

A prominent feature of the typical tavern was the sturdily locked, well-stocked bar. Frequent passers-through were directed to keep track of all that they'd consumed, to be paid for at a final reckoning. Because sometimes these topers drank by the pint and sometimes by the quart, the tavern keeper would sing out to them at the time of settling the charge, "Mind your p's and q's!" He meant that they should tally care-

32

The People's Line--Take care of the Locomotive
Sold at 104 Nassau, and 18 Division Streets, New-York.

fully the amounts due for pints and quarts. The phrase has somewhat altered its meaning in recent times, but p's and q's still call us to a reckoning.

Tavern keepers thus became key players in the whole new business of transportation (which could hardly have been considered anything like an organized profession in the early 1700s). By 1800, when young Martin Van Buren of Kinderhook, New York, was considering how to shape his career, he was told by responsible family members that, for an ambitious, upcountry striver, there were but two options: become either a lawyer or a tavern keeper. Both would provide rank and security in the community.

The Fate of the National Road

And so it appeared that America was ready—ready with road-building techniques, with convenient vehicles for freight and passengers, and with friendly taverns along the

33

Henry Clay won fame—and some ridicule, right—for his advocacy of the "American System," a national program for internal improvements.

way—to construct a reliable route to the West. It would be a turnpike, as economically productive as the Lancaster Pike. It would be the National Pike.

This was indeed a great and popular and timely undertaking, a significant triumph for Thomas Jefferson and Henry Clay in their respective times. Built, as described, on the remnants of Braddock's old Cumberland Road, it expressed the spirit of the young republic. But for all its excellence, the pike faltered and failed, apparently incapable of reaching its Mississippi River goal. As it limped across Ohio into Indiana in the 1830s, construction became sloppier and slower, the road's surface now being of gravel rather than crushed rock.

The National Road became a symbol not of how Americans might unite their nation by advanced transportation technology but of why the divided nation would fail to advance swiftly into the industrial age. To Americans today, reviewing that historic disappointment, the vital question seems to be whether a democracy, with all its special-interest pressures, can ever rise above the competing interests of the respective states and create a transportation system (or a housing policy or an environmental program) that benefits all.

High cost was, understandably, a major reason for the National Road's slowdown, the absolutely unheard-of sum of $7 million having been required from the federal government. Then there was the length, an unprecedented eight hundred miles through forest and across major rivers: Was such a giant step really feasible? But it was the political nature of the National Road that caused it so much difficulty. This was not only the matter of constitutionality—which caused President James Monroe to veto a bill for the "preservation and repair" of the National Road in 1822—but also of opposed regional interests. Why should it be acceptable to New Englanders or Southerners to have all those millions spent on a road for the primary benefit of the West?

Monroe's veto signaled a reversal of the federal attitude toward the National Pike. Once the most beloved project of the Jeffersonians, the country's most impressive road was then cast aside as a major threat to the doctrine of states' rights, looming as almost Hamiltonian in its manifestation of an all-powerful, central government. Behind Monroe's small-state theory and his strict interpretation of the Constitution lay another element: the issue of whether the federal government should rival private corporations by undertaking such capital-intensive ventures as the National Road. The Jeffersonians thought not, as did the new conservatives (later called Whigs), for different reasons.

It was at this point that Henry Clay rose so magnificently to the challenge, convincing the Congress to pass another key bill in support of the National Road and persuading Monroe to sign it in 1825 (the last act of his administration). Thereafter, with Clay at the helm and malleable John Quincy Adams in the White House, eight more bills were passed to maintain the road and carry it westward. A crisis had, apparently, been passed.

But still the National Road limped on, harassed, finally reaching the dreary, Kaskaskia

River port of Vandalia, Illinois (50 miles east of St. Louis on the Mississippi) in 1852. By that time, railroad interests were asserting themselves across the land, asking two undeniably legitimate questions: Could not better progress toward western objectives be made, more cheaply, by railroad than by turnpike? And why shouldn't the railroads be aided by the beneficent federal government? By the time Andrew Jackson took over the reins of government (1829), both of those questions had been heard in the halls of Congress. The president pondered them, and the destiny of American transportation hung in the balance.

Within little more than a year of assuming the presidency, Jackson wrote such a strongly worded veto of a proposed turnpike that few doubted the direction of federal policy. The vetoed turnpike was an important one, connecting Kentucky's heartland with the Ohio River at Maysville, downstream from Wheeling. But it seemed clear to the president that, as an enterprise within one state's borders, the Maysville Turnpike could not properly receive assistance from the treasury of the United States (which was then, as it happened, severely pressed and under demand from a variety of sources). Based on those constitutional grounds, Jackson's 1830 veto seemed solid; the flow of federal funds to highway builders had been turned off, with all the finality of a locked spigot.

The president did support road building to the extent of approving ten successive bills to push the National Road farther west (for the massive total of $3.75 million). But he spoke increasingly against federal ownership of and participation in such costly enterprises. His most notable effort for the pike was to transfer respective sections of it to the ownership of states through which it ran. One could almost hear the national government washing its hands of direct involvement in transportation.

Jackson had made his decision to veto federal assistance to the private Kentucky corporation that was undertaking the Maysville Pike because of his own political beliefs and on the insistence of what we would call today

his economic advisors. Those latter-day Jeffersonians feared that this use of federal funds, approved by the Congress, would signal to all American corporations that the government was on their side—the side of entrepreneurial capitalism—and no longer on the side of the agrarian, people's economy.

There had been a time in the awkward, problematical growth of the American economy when government assistance was needed for any large-scale, public undertaking (be it Jefferson's Louisiana Purchase or George Washington's desired canal along the Potomac). There simply did not exist enough private, domestic capital to finance internal improvements. But by the 1830s, at the time of Jackson's Maysville veto, that condition had passed; no longer was there an identification between private interest (meaning the business community) and public action.

De Tocqueville had warned, "The love of wealth [seems to be] at the bottom of all that Americans do." Conversely, scorn for anything that loses money seems a part of our national makeup. As it became clear that turnpikes were too expensive to be good business, and as the antibusiness descendants of Jefferson and Jackson commenced withholding federal funds from public road-building and canal programs, the future of extensive land transportation fell into other hands.

Unfortunately, the magnificently projected National Road, based on the attractive precedent of the Lancaster Pike, would be forgotten or remembered only as a bad example. While government at all levels would be responsible for capitalizing some 70 percent of the nation's canal systems built in the 1830s and 1840s, it would support no more than 30 percent of the railroads built in the era immediately before the Civil War. Thus Uncle Sam gradually withdrew from the business of helping Americans move across their land, deigning to give that business neither direction nor standards. The federal government would never take the leadership in transportation again—not until the subject was, once more, interstate highways, in the middle of the next century.

JOHN FITCH'S PLAN FOR WESTWARD WATERWAYS

Opposite: A bronze Robert Fulton, famous steamboat in hand, stands above the Library of Congress's Main Reading Room.

The American dreamers and inventors who changed American transportation at the beginning of the eighteenth century have always appeared somewhat shadowed. Unlike Thomas Jefferson or Benjamin Franklin, the varied geniuses of this new generation—New England's John Fitch and Philadelphia's Oliver Evans, the Erie Canal's De Witt Clinton and the Mississippi River's Captain Henry Shreve—never basked in the bright sunshine of eternal approbation. Yet these were the creative forces behind the great technological leap taken by this nation soon after the Revolution: the leap that connected East with West and North with South.

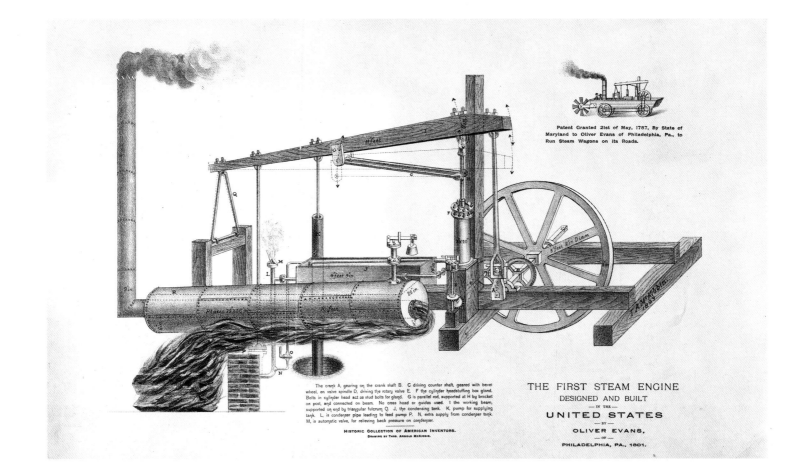

The crank A, gearing on the crank shaft B. C driving counter shaft, geared with bevel wheel, on valve spindle D, driving the rotary valve E. F the cylinder headstuffing box gland. Bolts in cylinder head act as stud bolts for gland. G is parallel rod, supported at H by bracket on post, and connected on beam. No cross head or guides used. I the working beam, supported on end by triangular fulcrum Q. J, the condensing tank. K, pump for supplying tank. L, is condenser pipe leading to feed pump P. N, extra supply from condenser tank. M, is automatic valve, for relieving back pressure on condenser.

HISTORIC COLLECTION OF AMERICAN INVENTORS.
DRAWING BY THOS. ARNOLD MCKIBBIN.

Patent Granted 21st of May, 1787, By State of Maryland to Oliver Evans of Philadelphia, Pa., to Run Steam Wagons on its Roads.

THE FIRST STEAM ENGINE
DESIGNED AND BUILT
— IN THE —
UNITED STATES
— BY —
OLIVER EVANS,
— OF —
PHILADELPHIA, PA., 1801.

W. Rawle

THE ABORTION

OF THE

YOUNG STEAM ENGINEER'S GUIDE:

CONTAINING

An investigation of the principles, construction and powers of Steam Engines.
A description of a Steam Engine on new principles, rendering it much more powerful, more simple, less expensive, and requiring much less fuel than an engine on the old construction.

A description of a Machine, and its principles, for making Ice and cooling water in large quantities, in hot countries, to make it palatable and wholesome for drinking, by the power of Steam: invented by the author.
A description of four other patented inventions.

ILLUSTRATED WITH FIVE ENGRAVINGS.

BY OLIVER EVANS, OF PHILADELPHIA,
AUTHOR OF THE YOUNG MILLWRIGHT AND MILLER'S GUIDE.

PHILADELPHIA:
PRINTED FOR THE AUTHOR BY FRY AND KAMMERER.
1805.

Although Great Britain and other European nations contributed many of the concepts and tools that helped us advance into this phase of the industrial era, it was unmistakably native genius that adapted those key devices to the special, transcontinental needs of our young republic. The particular contributions, the inventions, of those natives can now be seen as quite as remarkable for their difficulty to market as for their ingenuity.

Oliver Evans, if mentioned at all in history books, is given a fleeting nod for his invention of the automated flour mill. But he had an amazing vision of steam-powered vehicles which his contemporaries found inappropriate, inapplicable to their place and time, an indication that the country boy's mind was overtaxed.

What caused his Philadelphia critics most indignation was Evans's proposal to the Pennsylvania legislature in 1786 that he be given a monopoly on *steam-powered wagons* within the state. The apparently deluded inventor then said he would bet anyone $3,000 that he could create a steam-driven carriage that would at-

tain a speed of fifteen miles per hour. "I was then as confident as I am now," he wrote later, "that such velocity could be given to carriages … I am still willing to make a steam carriage that will run fifteen miles an hour, on good, level railways." Finding no takers, he doubled the bet.

Who could blame the skeptics? The future could not be seen any better then than now, but exciting changes were imminent. What possible role steam might play in the development of American transportation, whether on land or on sea, was about to be resolved. That was central in the drama of how Americans, not by muscle alone but with a mechanical boost, might take many miles at a bound.

He Dreamed of Steamboats on Western Rivers

Certainly John Fitch did everything he could to force his fellow countrymen to see that steamboats—his steamboats—were the only way to conquer the great distances of the transmontane West. He preached with both passion and reason that the only way to follow the westward-reaching rivers to the internationally contested Mississippi Valley was by a boat that could fight the currents mechanically.

Though he became acquainted with Oliver Evans and other creative contemporaries when operating in the nation's capital of Philadelphia during the years after the Revolution, Fitch had been born in rural Windsor, Connecticut, in 1743. Like many another ingenious Yankee, he'd learned early in life how to repair guns and clocks; he had an instinctive and inventive, if undereducated, way with things mechanical. His matured talents, we can now see, may not have been unusual but they were extraordinarily well-focused.

He had a rough edge, however. In his midtwenties he had quarreled with his wife and deserted his family. Looking back at that rude act in later years—when the Philadelphia Library asked the publicly recognized inventor to leave his papers in its care—he wrote, "I

Flag flying, paddles dipping, John Fitch's steamboat moves upriver past Philadelphia on August 22, 1787, in the drawing above. Inset in a plan for Oliver Evans's first steam engine, opposite above, the artist portrayed Evans's steam dredge. On the title page of a guide for steam engineers, below, Evans wrote a beseeching note, opposite.

Copyright 1907.   S.Hollyer.

"The Devil going upriver in a sawmill!" exclaimed one observer of Fulton's steamship on the Hudson in 1807, above. Opposite: A later Fulton steamboat, named *Paragon*, had enclosed paddlewheels but still retained sails for extra speed.

know of nothing so perplexing and vexatious to a man of feelings, as a turbulent Wife and Steamboat building. I experienced the former, and quit in season; and had I been in my right sences [sic], I should undoubtedly have treated the latter in the same manner."

Leaving home behind him, he had become a roustabout on a coasting vessel, then a clock repairer and silversmith in various coastal cities. But after the attacking British wrecked his shop in Trenton early in the Revolution, he became a purveyor of tobacco and beer to the American troops. Setting forth with his wagon from a new headquarters near Baltimore, he grossed as much as £150 per week, making a small and apparently honest fortune. When peace finally arrived, his only problem was how to translate those war profits into something permanent.

Roaming into Daniel Boone's Kentucky, he viewed with wonder the breadth and openness of the Ohio River. Hitching a ride on a riverboat, he found himself swept downstream, where he grounded on one of the many uncharted shoals. Captured by a band of waiting Indians—who tended to regard all these incursive, newly victorious Americans as enemies—Fitch struggled to survive. He was of course a whittler, able to make little toys and horn carvings; and thus he amused his captors. Eventually they sold him to their late allies, the British who still remained palisaded at Detroit.

Hardly pausing to recuperate, John Fitch was soon back on the Ohio River. And there, even while hearing of (and scorning) reports that some inventors back in Philadelphia had been talking of steam vehicles for land travel, he dreamed of and worked on a model for a steam-powered riverboat. Simultaneously, he sought a commission as surveyor. Tactless and impolitic and lacking connections, he failed to win the appointment. Still, he knew that he must be on the right track with his steamboat idea. How else would the nation claim the West?

Back he came to the capital with his inspiring (though admittedly not original) idea of a long-distance steamship.

He took the presumptuous step of presenting a model of his proposed craft to Philadelphia's American Philosophical Society, in whose halls it may still be seen. Then, searching for a mechanic experienced enough actually to build this imagined steamboat, he fortunately encountered a watchmaker-engineer of German descent named Henry Voight.

"That genius Voight," Fitch called him, marveling at his colleague's skill in shaping machinery from wood and iron and copper; further, "To his inventive genius alone, I am indebted for the improvement in our mode of creating steam." And the taming of steam was, of course, the prime technical problem. In the early years of the century, England's pioneer scientists Thomas Newcomen, Thomas Savery, and James Watt had probed the principles of steam expansion (it requires sixteen hundred times the amount of space as the water from which it is formed). Systems had been devised which—by means of condensers, flywheels, and mercury gauges—permitted steam power to be harnessed and applied to a huge, effective, but stationary engine.

After the American Revolution, there were only two or three of these heavy industrial steam engines in North America. But there were two immigrants—the Irish scientist Christopher Colles in New York and the English architect-engineer Benjamin Latrobe in Philadelphia—who had the knowledge and skill to transfer to American minds an understanding of those steam engines' dynamics.

One of the minds so influenced was James Rumsey's. He, an ingenious Baltimorean, had

40

met Colles in the early 1780s and had pondered the application of steam to the propulsion of boats. After some years of experimentation, Rumsey designed a craft that was driven forward by jets of steam-driven water blasting out the stern. This somewhat bizarre invention was demonstrated on the waters of the Potomac River to the delight of assembled dignitaries and the scientific community (including Jefferson and Franklin) in 1787. Jefferson, no mean tinkerer himself, called Rumsey America's "greatest mechanical genius."

Forever afterward, Rumsey has represented the South in the very important matter of who invented the American steamboat. Unfortunately, however, he died before his boat could be tested in the commercial market.

In the same year as James Rumsey's demonstration on the Potomac, John Fitch and Henry Voight commenced their operations on the Delaware River, upstream from Philadelphia at the little village of Neshaminy. There they built a small skiff, in which could be seated a steam engine with a three-inch cylinder. The next step was to devise a powerful drive system.

Fitch had in mind a contraption of conveyor belt and oars which he called a "paddlewheel." To construct it he and Voight (in Fitch's words) "taxed the skills of blacksmiths and mechan-

ics to the limit." The design called for six oars in two pairs of three on each side of the boat; these were alternately raised and lowered as if teams of invisible rowers were at work. Fitch described it this way in 1786:

Each revolution of the axel-tree moves twelve oars five and a half feet; as six oars come out of the water, six more enter the water, which makes a stroke of about eleven feet each revolution [of the conveyor belt]. The oars are perpendicular, and make a stroke similar to the paddle of a canoe.

It worked!

Fitch was eager not only to prove to skeptics that his ideas for steam propulsion had been correctly worked out but also to win both financial backing and broad monopolies on steamboats across the land. Most fortuitous, it seemed to him, was the fact that Philadelphia in that summer of 1787 was site of the Constitutional Convention. So he announced that on August 22 he and Voight would demonstrate this splendid steamboat of theirs, the steamboat that had sufficient power to propel the nation to its destiny beyond the mountains.

The capital city on that August day was sweltering, crowded, bored with anything new.

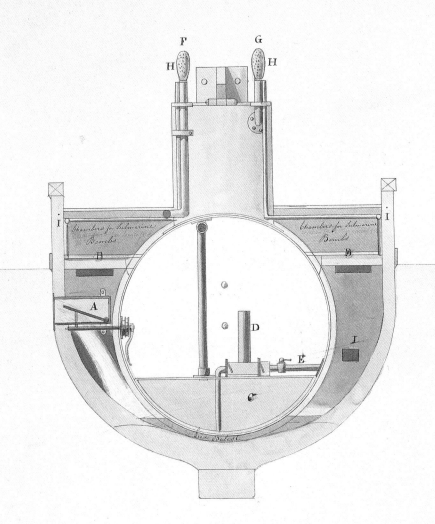

and insisted that he recognize his efforts, the grand old statesman dug into his pockets and managed to find but five or six dollars. Affronted, Fitch refused them.

Nor was his boat's performance on the Delaware particularly convincing to other Philadelphians. Paddles whirring maniacally and splashing mightily allowed the craft to move through the waves at about four knots. The supporters whom Fitch had brought to the point of watching the demonstration voiced doubts that the boat would ever move faster, and surely more speed than that would be needed to breast the westward rivers. Many of them declined further investments, agreeing with Franklin that Rumsey's craft was probably superior.

Enough supporters were impressed, however, so that Fitch (who tried to attract investors in his enterprise by selling $20 shares) raised nearly $8,000—the greatest amount yet granted to an American inventor. Fitch also secured "sole and exclusive" rights for steam navigation from the states of New Jersey, Delaware, Pennsylvania, and Virginia—even from New York, which had its own contenders for steamboat rights. The Virginia patent had one tricky clause in it, however, specifying that Fitch had to have boats of

Fulton also pushed his ideas for submarines, above, and floating batteries for the War of 1812. After the building of the Erie Canal—sentimentalized in the sketch opposite—canals boomed and day-trippers could enjoy canal rides, as in the advertisement at right.

One citizen had notified Thomas Jefferson of the advertised appearance of a steamboat. He wrote that "one Fitch" had spent much money in the project and had "heated his imagination so as to be himself a steam engine." The fact is, Fitch was not much liked in Philadelphia; he was a Unitarian and he was uncivilly outspoken in his liberal political views. He was described as "tall, gaunt, shabby, excitable, almost incoherent."

Benjamin Franklin, having been impressed by Rumsey's scientific approach, was inclined to doubt both the theory and the practice of Fitch's system; most of all, he suspected that this new boat would be too expensive and ungainly to serve its purpose. He decided he had better things to do on that afternoon than watch another awkward example of Yankee toymaking. Further, when Fitch accosted him

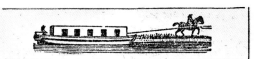

twenty tons—boats far larger than his trial craft—functioning satisfactorily by a certain date.

It was essential for Fitch to deliver on that clause, otherwise most of the territory west of the Appalachians and south of the Ohio River (still designated as Virginia) would be lost to him. To make him even more apprehensive, Fitch had not been able to win an exclusive license from Spanish authorities for the territories west of the Mississippi River. His whole financial scheme depended on access to western rivers controlled by those authorities.

While hurrying to improve his engine and make money from his existing craft, Fitch also commenced construction of a new and larger steamboat. In the autumn of 1788 he carried thirty passengers up the Delaware from Philadelphia to Burlington, New Jersey in but three hours and ten minutes. The next spring, operating with a larger craft, he initiated regular timetable runs between those Delaware River ports. The improved engine that he and Voight

had struggled over now pushed the vessel at seven knots. Although he could still not beat the time of rival stagecoaches and failed to attract sufficient passengers to make money, the enterprise seemed full of promise.

Fitch wrote happily of himself and his partner, "We reigned Lord High Admirals of the Delaware … . Thus had been effected, by little Johnny Fitch and Harry Voight, one of the greatest and most useful arts that has ever been introduced into the world; and although the world and my country does not thank me for it, yet it gives me heartfelt satisfaction."

Soon thereafter Fitch was steering his newly constructed boat down the Delaware from the shipyard. Named *Perseverance*, she was large enough to fulfill the Virginia performance demands—Fitch's total gamble. Suddenly, he and his crew were struck by an overwhelming gale at Petty's Island, just north of the capital. Waves smashed the hull against the island's shores. The battering was remorseless; eventually the

New York State's Erie Canal, originally built for freight traffic, proved popular for westward travelers like the couple on the towpath in the scene at right. Engineers continued to admire the Erie long after its 1825 completion; the studies opposite were drafted by a West Point student in the 1850s.

boat and all the invested money that it represented sank out of sight.

Despite Fitch's pertinacity in improving his designs and his repeated attempts to gain new funds here and abroad on the basis of a 1790 U.S. patent (one of the first granted), he went on from disappointment to tragedy. He kept improving the design of his steamboat, experimenting with a screw propeller and sidewheels. But he'd lost his audience; he was viewed as a tiresome crank. Finally he fled to the Kentucky territories where he'd staked a claim after the Revolution. By then, aged fifty-five, he was drinking heavily cursing his fates and the treacheries of others. Seeing no way to emerge from his misfortunes, he swallowed rat poison in July 1798, ending his talented life in agonized despair.

A Dinosaur of a Dredge

As for Fitch's even more talented acquaintance, Oliver Evans (whose automated flour mill was granted a U.S. patent in 1790), he too failed to be recognized as the progenitor of the American steamboat. Young Evans—whose father (like Henry Ford's father) considered the boy "cracked" and wished he would pursue more "remunerative tasks" than steam inventions—kept wondering if there were not a way to improve upon the "low-pressure" steam engines that were imported from England. After many experiments, he developed the condenserless "high-pressure" steam engine— far more compact and useful for boats or carriages than the British design.

By 1804, when Oliver Evans's high-pressure engine had received its own patent, he determined to demonstrate what steam might do for American transportation. Putting his twelve-horsepower steam engine into one of the strangest vehicles ever seen, an amphibious dredge with the dinosaurian name of *Orukter Amphibolous*, he rumbled through Philadelphia's staid streets into Center Square. The steam engine hissed and thumped, the

44

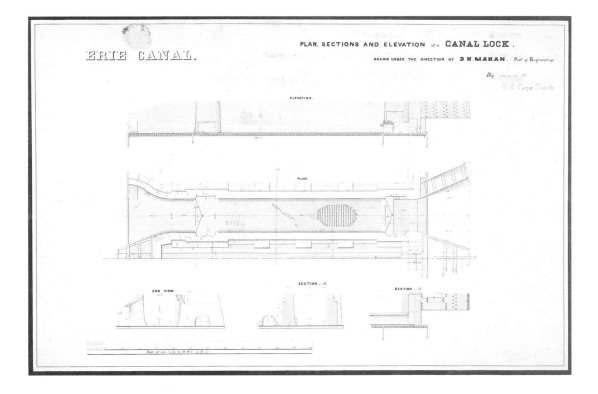

PLAN, SECTIONS AND ELEVATION of a CANAL LOCK.

DRAWN UNDER THE DIRECTION OF **D.H. MAHAN.** Prof. of Engineering.

By

U.S. Corps Cadets.

ELEVATION.

PLAN.

END VIEW.   SECTION ... III   SECTION ... IV

metal wheels chewed the pavement as mothers dragged their children out of the way. This was all an effort on Evans's part to dramatize the feasibilty of steam vehicles on land or sea and to capture the attention of investors. He also intended to charge onlookers twenty-five cents a glance.

To his chagrin, Philadelphia deigned not to notice as the dredge circled the square and rumbled along to the Schuylkill River. Even when the dredge splashed into the river and successfully breasted its current, the audience remained unimpressed. America was simply not ready for steam-powered transportation—certainly not when presented by such impolite characters as John Fitch and Oliver Evans.

When, on the other hand, the distinguished Robert Fulton—artist and engineer, handsome and well-married friend of the mighty—sailed his steamboat up the Hudson River from New York to Albany in 1807, the event was hailed as the wondrous beginning of a new era. The excitement of Fulton's feat endured for years: at the end of the century Henry Adams (scion of the presidential family and author of the *History of the United States*) saluted August 17th, 1807, rather than July 4th, 1776, as the true beginning of this country, the commence-

ment of our independence. A statue of the inspired Fulton may be seen among those of other American geniuses in the dome above the Library of Congress's Main Reading Room, marking the inventor's historic prominence.

Why was Fulton's trip upriver so popular when Fitch's and Evans's were not? Was it the fact that Fulton had been scientifically advanced enough to test his boat in a 106-foot tank that would do credit to modern naval architecture? Was it the elegance of his boat's structure (a shallow, low-resistance hull and a smokestack that towered thirty feet above the deck)? A modern sociologist would reply, No, this isn't a matter of higher technique or superior product; it's merely one of those discontinuities we should be prepared for in the lurching pattern of social history.

The Strange Allure of Canals

During that historic gap—the lapse between the Fitch-Evans failures with steamboats and the Fulton successes—the country went, as reported at the time, "canal crazy." Beginning soon after the Revolution, increasing before and after the War of 1812, and peaking in the 1830s and 1840s, the surge of canal

The greatest American expedition of the early nineteenth century: Lewis and Clark's journey up the Missouri to the Northwest coast is traced on fellow traveler Robert Frazer's hand-drawn map of 1807, opposite. The explorers first sailed by keel boat. They and other officials also used long-range native canoes like those in the painting above.

building proved that certain radically minded Americans would try anything to get themselves West.

English engineers had offered this watery solution to the problem of transporting goods inexpensively across the landscape. The canals built on behalf of the Duke of Bridgewater had succeeded in uniting England's coal mines with her industrial centers (thereby making the duke a fortune). So, mused certain American leaders, perhaps that mode and not steam was the most feasible way to unite the West with East of the not-yet United States.

Their musings turned into a massive program. By the time of the Civil War, Americans in virtually every northern state east of the Mississippi had built a four thousand-mile system of inter-connecting canals. Close to $188 million was spent on this network—which grew to be twice as extensive as Great Britain's canal system. It was the greatest waterway system in the world, a magnificent accomplishment; yet the building of it left the respective American states more than $60 million in the red (a load of indebtedness that crushed a number of them). And, most ironically, this amazing and truly fabulous network of canals was built at a time when the steam-powered railroads were believed by many to be a less expensive, more effective mode of overland transportation.

Economists today recall with despair the wasteful excesses of the canal era. Columbia University's Carter Goodrich, in his classic study of this era, concluded that the building of canals had clearly been a "mislocation of economic resources" for the United States in those tender years of growth.

Nevertheless, the emplacement of this immense though fragile network of canals—which would be complemented by, then replaced by, the steamboats and the railroads—enabled the North to become an industrial power of sufficient might to command the world's respect and even to win the bloodiest war of U.S. history.

Furthermore, it was during and because of the canal era that Americans started to move across their land in great numbers. The canals launched us on our destiny of perpetual mobil-

state's capital for $.75. There was no surprise, of course, that moving goods on water was less costly and easier than overland transportation (thanks mostly to the physical fact of less resistance), but the astonishing economic advantage of that saving in shipping costs to all of New York's enterprises shocked and challenged rival states.

Astonishing too was the success of the state's canal board in deriving such rich revenues from the waterway (and from the special tax on salt produced near Syracuse) that, on their balance sheets, income exceeded expenses by 1826. The initial investment of

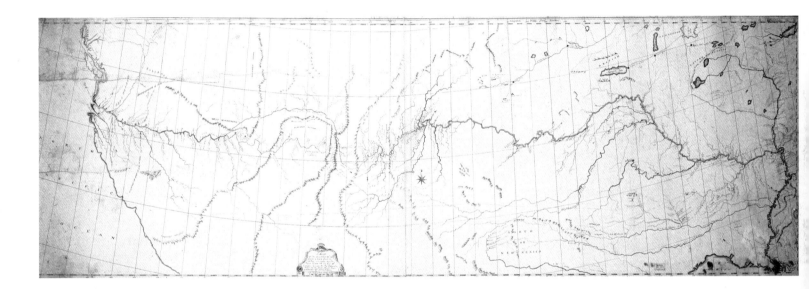

ity. And the best answer to the cruel question of how we could have committed ourselves to the folly of building a $188-million system that would become obsolete so fast is, simply, that at first the canals worked so extraordinarily well. The first major American canal—the Erie Canal, which connected the Hudson River by way of the Mohawk Valley with the Great Lakes and the midwestern waterways at Buffalo—was such a winner, financially and politically, that everyone wanted to emulate it.

After the opening of the Erie Canal in 1825, the cost of shipping a ton of farmer's produce from Rochester to East Coast markets dropped from $100 to $5; a barrel of flour, for which the shipping cost from Rochester to Albany used to be $3, now could be shipped to the

$8 million was entirely paid back within ten years. Land values across the state boomed by the millions, encouraging a wave of speculation that would later cause much grief. Formerly humble towns grown rich because of the canal rechristened themselves with classical names like Rome and Syracuse; on their slopes opulent Greek Revival mansions sprang from the mud like so many spring flowers.

This blossoming should not be remembered, however, as a swift and easy accomplishment. Not only had efforts to connect the eastern and western parts of New York State by canal been foiled since colonial times and at the end of the eighteenth century, but also DeWitt Clinton's successful campaign to build his "Big Ditch" met with nearly every conceivable setback and obstacle. The U.S. Congress, led by South Carolina's John Calhoun, approved a funding bill to construct the proposed Erie Canal in 1817. But President Madison unhesitatingly vetoed the bill, citing constitutional problems—although he had approved no less than six laws aiding the Cumberland Road.

Other mighty voices were raised in objection to Clinton's proposal. The eminent John Stevens of New Jersey—who, though creator of a successful, twin-screwed steam ferry between New York City and Hoboken in 1811, had shifted his attention from steamboating to railroading—pointed out that it made no sense to build such a costly, primitive thing as a canal when railroads would soon be crossing the country. Some people believed him. Even in his own New York State, where Clinton finally persuaded long-time opponent Martin Van Buren to side with him, the idea of the state financing the canal on the basis of its own financial resources seemed far too daring to conservatives. The integrity of the project was constantly challenged by those who wanted to build the canal no farther than Lake Ontario.

To imagine going to Lake Erie—and from there to the Mississippi valley—was simply beyond the horizon of many easterners. The proud merchants of New York City were particularly blind to the values of being able to reach the Erie (though they would, as it happened, benefit enormously from the canal's traffic, brought down the Hudson). Certainly there was cause for doubt that the 363-mile-long canal could ever be built, both because of the difficulties of the route and because of the lack of engineering talent in the United States at the beginning of the nineteenth century.

Recognizing that attempts by previous, eighteenth-century canal builders (including George Washington, along the Potomac River) had been frustrated by limited knowledge of technical solutions, Clinton and his committee had sent the talented Canvass White and two other willing students to England to absorb what they could. It was White who, on return, discovered a native clay in New York State that could be made into the hydraulic cement contractors needed to complete the canal's eighty-three locks. It was other ingenious New Yorkers who figured out how to build the monumental set of five double locks at Lockport (on which locks, in the words of a local newspaper, "two thousand Irishmen were working night and day").

Yet another team of New Yorkers figured out how to surmount the final, seventy-five-foot height of the Niagara Escarpment which blocked the way to Lake Erie. This was very much a homemade effort, undertaken with more courage than common sense; a chance taken on the future, all the more remarkable for its improbability.

Wedding of the Waters

When the triumphant Governor Clinton and his flotilla of garlanded vessels traveled down the completed canal in November 1825, with cannonades all the way from Buffalo to Albany, then down to New York City and back, he was joined by a mighty assemblage of congratulatory personalities. President John Quincy Adams consented to address the throng at City Hall; former Presidents John Adams, Thomas Jefferson, and James Madison also took part in the parades and fireworks. For all the homegrown char-

For the taming of westward rivers in the days of barges and flatboats, African-American boatmen provided strength and skill, below. River travelers on steamboats also took risks. The tragic 1845 destruction of *Swallow*, opposite, in which forty perished, was not considered unusual.

acter of the canal's making, this was recognized as a national event.

As whistles blasted, horns tooted, and the forts in New York harbor let fly with more salutes, Clinton finally felt the surges of the Atlantic Ocean rocking his canal boat, the *Seneca Chief*. With him he had brought kegs of Lake Erie's waters; he stated that by pouring water from one of the kegs into the ocean he was symbolizing all "which has been accomplished between our Mediterranean Sea and the Atlantic Ocean in about eight years." He then prayed that "the God of the Heavens and of the Earth [might] smile propitiously on this work and render it subservient to the best interests of the human race." This "wedding of the waters" was seen by people of the day as a turning point in the history of the nation, and, indeed, of the world.

One factor not anticipated in all the euphoria was that, although the Erie Canal would indeed live up to its expectations as a great carrier of freight, the major economic change would come from the carrying of people. The freight traffic, on "line barges," was as heavy as expected: Even before the entire canal was finished, the fortunate millers of Rochester could ship thousands more barrels of their flour to the coast, reaching an annual total of ten thousand barrels by 1823. But the moving of people—unexpected by early planners and entrepreneurs and barge-builders—became an even more significant change: By the mid-1840s (the peak of the canal era) nearly 100,000 people each year were moving along the canal to Buffalo and on into the West.

The fanciest passengers sped along at four miles per hour on gaily painted "packet boats."

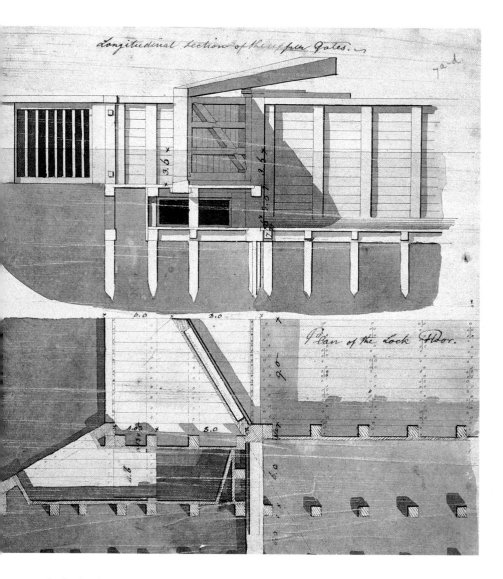

Longitudinal Section of the upper Gates.

Plan of the Lock Floor.

At the beginning of the nineteenth century, U.S. engineers had to learn from foreign tutors, led by England's Benjamin Henry Latrobe—whose drawing of a proper canal lock appears above. Later Americans heedlessly pushed technology to extremes. In an 1870 contest of steamboats on the Mississippi, the *R.E. Lee* powered up the Mississippi—in a race like that shown opposite—in a record-breaking three days, eighteen hours.

In fair weather they could ride atop the slightly arched roof, while watching out for the low bridges that had been built to allow farmers to get back and forth between fields on either side of the canal. Less affluent passengers—including a new generation of immigrants fleeing from Europe's plagues and revolutions—rode on jam-packed passenger barges, seeking new lives in the ever-beckoning West. Pilgrims all, they shared the essential American experience of having traveled to get here, of continuing to travel to get farther along.

It is to be expected, therefore, that this experience found its way into popular songs like "Low Bridge, Everybody Down!" and into legends of brawling Irish and German canal workers. Burl Ives, balladeer of our own day, was wont to delight audiences with his rendition of this authentic song of canallers:

> Oh the Eri-e was a-rising.
> And the gin was getting low,
> And I scarcely think we'll get a drink
> Till we get to Buffalo,
> Till we get to Buffalo.

We are inclined to recall the canal era not so much through history as through legend and myth, through the emphatically American folk songs of travelers. Nonetheless, neither the mythic quality of the Erie Canal nor the low-tech quality of its construction should obscure for us its historical significance.

Certainly in its own time, New York's Erie Canal made an enormous impact. In Philadelphia the cry went up that Pittsburgh was "doomed" because most midwestern traffic would now no longer flow through that port but through Buffalo. In Ohio, Indiana, Illinois, and even Wisconsin, legislators cast caution aside and voted for imitative canal systems financed by enormous state debts. In Massachusetts, a proposal to build a $10 million canal across the entire length of the state to the Hudson was barely defeated; wiser heads determined that a railroad would be more sensible. (It eventually became the Boston & Albany, America's first successful long-distance rail route.)

In Maryland a race began between canal and railroad to reach the mountains. The

canal was a revived version of George Washington's yearned-for canal up the Potomac; but this one, the Chesapeake & Ohio Canal, would, wisely, follow its own engineered channel and not the river bed on the way to Cumberland. The railroad was christened the Baltimore & Ohio. In 1828, work on both routes commenced on July 4 (always the favored date for the commencement of such national endeavors), with President John Quincy Adams wielding a not particularly effective shovel to begin the digging of the canal. Legend has it that, when the presidential shovel struck a root and would go no farther, Adams smiled for the first and only time in his administration. The canal, not completed until 1850 (eight years after the railroad reached the same terminal), would cost $12 million; yet

it functioned adequately, even if in the shadow of the railroad, until 1924.

Somehow Over the Alleghenies

Evaluated in terms of greatest risk taken—possibly greatest foolishness committed—Pennsylvania's "Main Line" Canal must win the prize. State legislators, hastening to organize a convention favoring canal construction at Harrisburg in 1826, pushed matters through so rapidly that ground was broken for their system on July 4 of that year. Certain cautionary words were heard from a brilliant Philadelphia engineer, an admirer of Jefferson named William Strickland (who had gone to England in 1825 and seen George Stephenson's *Rocket*, the first effective carriage-pulling locomotive). But, as the public cheered, thousands

51

and millions of dollars were voted for this bits-and-pieces canal which was to extend all the way to Pittsburgh, having somehow overcome the Alleghenies.

Despite its foolhardiness, Pennsylvania's central canal system would be a glorious accomplishment, a demonstration of what determined Americans could do when challenged. Having linked a number of natural waterways and horse-drawn railways and man-made canals from both the eastern and western ends of the entire route, the canal builders found themselves staring, in 1831, at the unyielding heights of Allegheny Mountain—a ridge that rose some 1,398 feet above the river town of Holidaysburg. No one had a coherent idea of how to get the canal boats up and over—or possibly through—the mountain. A four-mile tunnel was proposed, but no one possessed either the knowledge or the tools to build it. Then came the idea of a spiraling

roadway, up and around the mountain and down the other side; but the gradient would have been far too steep for any vehicles then known. Had all the money thus far—more than $8 million, the cost of the whole Erie Canal—been spent in vain?

The builders of the Main Line pressed on. Taking their cue from the recently completed Morris Canal of New Jersey, which pulled coal barges up over a 914-foot summit in the direction of New York harbor by means of an elegant inclined-plane system, they designed a combination of planes and levels. Flatbeds carrying the canal boats would be lifted up the five east-facing planes and lowered down the five western planes by stationary steam engines; they would be pulled along the intervening levels at first by horse teams then later by locomotives.

The many-leveled contraption was called the Allegheny Portage Railroad, parts of which are now being reconstructed as a national his-

Two major river ports visited by mid-nineteenth century steamboats: Louisville, Kentucky, below, located at the falls of the Ohio River; St. Louis, Missouri, opposite, was the booming gateway to the western prairies.

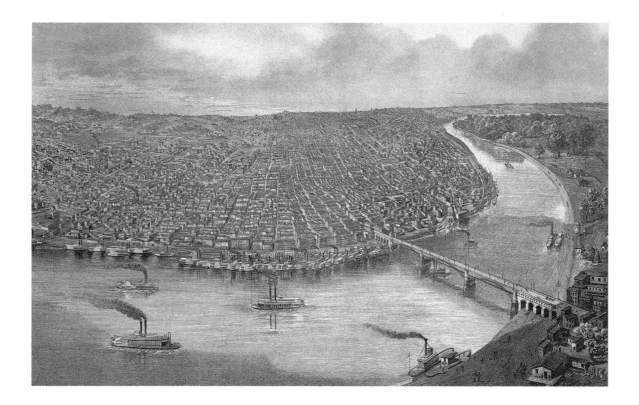

toric site. It functioned well enough, despite its makeshift engineering, to get the job done. During the Portage Railroad's busiest years, six cars were hauled up the inclines every hour; some thirty-five boats went through the western terminus (Johnstown, Pennsylvania) each day, full of passengers headed west. The travel time from Philadelphia to Pittsburgh was reduced from twenty-three days to four.

But the hardware used to achieve this transportation miracle was primitive, likely to snap or break, and causative of the kind of travel accidents that nineteenth-century Americans seemed to take quite calmly. In a three-day period in 1834 a particularly spectacular series of accidents took place. In one, a car at the head of Plane One broke loose and, "descending with incredible velocity," smashed into the posts of the shed at the foot. The only passenger, "a respectable stranger," was hurled sixty feet through the air into the Conemaugh River. Although railroad personnel were able to fish him out swiftly, he died the following evening from a fractured skull.

Ultimately, the Main Line Canal, whose complexities required passengers to change vehicles and mode of power thirty-three times during their passage, would last only ten years before being bought out and replaced by the Pennsylvania Railroad.

Boats for the Western Rivers

Canal boats that took Americans west in the 1830s and 1840s were old-fashioned things, designed along the lines of the so-called Durham Boats of the 1780s. Those heavy but shallow, sixty-foot craft had been built in order to float loads of iron down the Delaware River without going aground on the river's shoals. Adapted for use on one of Pennsylvania's earliest canals, the 1794 Schuylkill Canal, the boats retained their minimal, two-foot draft and their capacity to haul heavy loads.

Later canal boats, particularly the speedy packet boats, represented considerable refinements. Some showed remarkable diversity; the "sectional" boats used on the Main Line Canal, for example, could either be carried on rails as small units or be linked together in pairs as longer craft. The prevailing colors for most of the canal-boat hulls were green or brown, with the cabin houses painted and trimmed with red or white or blue (influenced, some think, by the Conestoga wagons' colors).

As late as 1909, when the above photo of the St. Louis waterfront was taken, steamboats still operated—despite the growth of railroads. Already their era had passed; never again would travelers see such opulence as on the gas-lit riverboats, opposite. Mark Twain called them "finer than any place on shore."

Specialized canal boats carried theatrical performers and barber shops; eventually steam-powered craft were seen on the canals, many of which were repair vessels.

Colorful or dingy, canal boats were all the offspring of America's ancient riverboats. And it was by riverboat that canal travelers were to continue their westward journeys, having reached the Ohio River or some other feeder of the Mississippi Valley by means of the eastern states' canal systems.

An amazing variety of craft could be found within the riverboat category—many of them being little more than rafts. A good raft was nothing to be scorned, however; some of them served as passenger-carrying vessels of considerable size, boasting cabin houses and enormous steering oars fore and aft for avoiding shoals and snags. As well as skiffs and scows

for local travel, there were also pole-boats, whose crews were armed with steel-tipped poles for controlling the down-stream passage.

Dugouts called *pirogues* (usually made from enormous beech trees) had been seen on northern rivers since the 1600s. The advantage of these and the grand canoes of the *voyageurs* was that they could be paddled, upstream as well as down. But on the more elaborate pole-boats, whose owners expected them to be brought home after the downstream voyage, reinforced walkways were added to the sides for the benefit of the muscular polesmen who had to push the craft against the current. These walkways came to be called *running boards*, a term later filched by automobile promoters.

During Abraham Lincoln's youth, in Illinois of the early 1800s, the accepted procedure was to construct a raft or pole-boat out of any wood and in any style you could think of and take a heap of farm produce for sale down to New Orleans—usually selling the planks of the boat in that exciting port—before walking all the way home.

It was by means of such crude riverboats that thousands upon thousands of Americans who had crossed the Appalachians on canal boats continued their pilgrimages, floating downriver to their western destinies. Even before the Louisiana Purchase, when knowledge of the western territories was scant, hundreds of river-craft would stream down the Ohio; during the year of 1778–79, more than five hundred craft arrived in or passed through Louisville on the Ohio, carrying an estimated twenty thousand people plus eight thousand horses, twenty-four hundred cattle, one thousand sheep, and seven hundred wagons. By the time of Lincoln's birth (1809) there were more than a million Americans living west of the Appalachians; in the first decade of the canal-boat era (the 1830s), that number increased to four million.

For moving far upstream against the current of North America's major interior rivers— the Missouri, the Platte, the Arkansas, the Red—something more mightily powered than the usual riverboat was necessary in the early years of the republic. Keelboats filled that need, although their proud captains eventually fought a losing battle against the incursive steamboats. Some keelboats were impressive, long-distance yachts with masts of forty or fifty feet and sails with sufficient authority to push the craft at four knots against the current. Originally, the boats had been constructed in Pittsburgh's yards during the hurry-up years after the Revolution. Besides sail power, their advantage over simpler river-craft was that the keel—a weighty underwater beam, running the length of the boat—helped the steersman stay on a determined course despite the swirling currents.

It was in one of these well-designed and equipped, uniquely American keelboats that Captain Meriwether Lewis and his friend William Clark were able to make their way up the Missouri River from St. Louis in 1804, the year after Jefferson's Louisiana Purchase. Their extraordinary, fifty-five-foot craft could be rowed by crewmen wielding twenty-two oars when the large square sail failed them. The

As travelers floated west across North America, they encountered rivers too shallow for steamboats—like the Platte, above, and the Gila, opposite. There the old flatboats still worked best.

sides were lined with watertight lockers behind which bulwark the men could find safety in case of an Indian attack; two small cannon, swivel guns located fore and aft, could then be unlimbered against the unlucky foe.

Given such a floating fortress, the explorers were able to keep sailing on confidently some miles after reaching the Three Forks of the Missouri (whose branches they named, for reasons of loyalty to the administration, after Jefferson, Gallatin, and Madison). Thereafter, having endured no attacks, they reached the crest of the Rockies by canoe and horse or foot.

It was amid this great diversity of river-craft (often indiscriminately called "arks"), before the arrival of the steamboats, that another species of American myth and legend began to develop—the tales of riverborne malefactors. That tradition would be developed to its fullest by Mark Twain in *The Adventures of Tom Sawyer* and *The Adventures of Huckleberry Finn*. Nor were all those tales totally fictitious. Pirates were a great and continuing threat: The death toll from gangs on the Ohio, Mississippi, and Natchez Trace between 1785 and 1805 was estimated to have exceeded two thousand women, men, and children.

The pirates' most notorious haunt was "Cave-in-Rock," an ugly spot near Shawneetown, Illinois, where rapids and whirlpools swirled above the junction of the Wabash and Ohio rivers. Pirates, stationed at midstream in dugouts, posed as pilots and offered to "git you through them riffles downstream." They did the job deftly, if gruffly, then urged the ark's master to "put ashore at that cave thar, 'cause it be a wondrous thing to see and it's got the sweetest drinkin' water in two hundred mile."

Inside the cave, blinking at its white limestone shimmer, the emigrants were shot down by other pirates hidden behind boulders.

Bodies and boat were looted, corpses were carried downstream and tossed overboard, and the ark itself was ferried down to the Cumberland or Tennessee rivers and sold for additional profits.

Fulfilling Fitch's Dream of Westward Steamboats

Robert Fulton, born near the transportation hub of Lancaster, Pennsylvania, in 1765, is popularly thought of as the inventor of the steamship (and therefore as conqueror of the western rivers). Pictures of his famous *Clermont* steaming triumphantly up the Hudson in 1807 were used to adorn plates, hatboxes, and wallpaper. Contemporaries delighted in repeating the story that one rustic Hudson River farmer had exclaimed that Fulton's *Clermont* looked like "the Devil going upriver in a sawmill!"

The fact was that Fulton's boat did not actually bear the memorable name *Clermont*; that name originally applied to the estate of Robert Livingston, the New York patron who possessed a steamboat monopoly on the Hudson (and who, by marriage, became related to as well as fascinated by the inventor). Also, Fulton did not actually invent the American steamboat, as seen earlier in this chapter. But such facts did nothing to cool the nation's love affair with the *Clermont* and her handsome, well-connected, and presumably genius-filled creator.

In both Europe and North America, Robert Fulton was able to capture the attention of the high and mighty. Forsaking any patriotic allegiance, he pushed his explosive devices (torpedoes, mines, etc.) in both France and England. In France he was granted an admiral's rank; in England he was so flattered that he found it difficult to return to his native land.

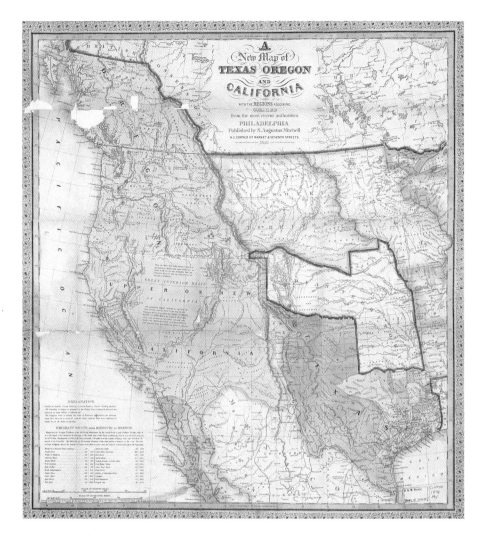

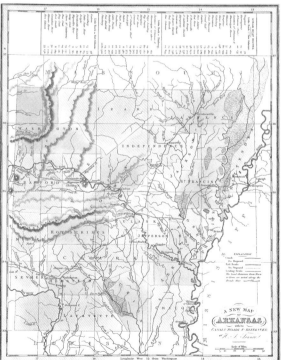

But once returned (in 1806), and having made his fortunate marriage—to an unfortunate bride, Livingston's young niece, who ultimately complained to that gentleman that Fulton paid her no attention—the young promoter-tinkerer concentrated with unquestioned creativity on perfecting his steamboat. What impressed Henry Adams and other students of American mores was that the Fulton-Livingston steamboats between New York and Albany ran on time, without accidents.

What impressed other, business-oriented observers was that these steamboats made money. Indeed, one wit remarked that the only trouble with Rumsey's and Evans's and Fitch's preceding steamboats was that they had run on the wrong rivers at the wrong time (the Potomac and the Delaware in the 1780s rather than on the Hudson a generation later). It was the length and consequent price of the ride from New York to Albany and the number of passengers who wanted to pay that price that allowed the Fulton-Livingston steamboats to turn profits. Along with those factors, the popular mind of the new generation had, somehow, been captured by the "romance of steam." Steam-powered craft on land and sea would, after the canal craze had abated, be the way Americans would travel.

Then entered another young and farsighted entrepreneur of travel: Nicholas Roosevelt (great-great-uncle of President Theodore). He proposed and worked out a partnership with Livingston and Fulton whereby he would develop traffic (under their monopoly) on the western rivers, thus fulfilling Fitch's dream. In the fall of 1809, Roosevelt and his bride, Lydia Latrobe, rode by Conestoga wagon to Pittsburgh, rented a keelboat, and sailed downstream to try to sell the concept of a Mississippi River steamboat line to merchant associations in Cincinnati, Louisville, Cairo, and New Madrid. Though skeptics (and keelboat enthusiasts) scoffed at the idea, it generated enough enthusiasm for Roosevelt to write home and order from Livingston a 116-foot boat, which he hoped to name the *New Orleans*.

The steam engine arrived by wagon in the spring of 1811; Fulton specified that this one-cylinder engine—the cylinder measuring thirty-four inches in diameter—should drive

paddlewheels placed amidships, just as with his boats on the Hudson. By August the *New Orleans* (also outfitted with mast and sails "just in case," as Roosevelt said) was launched and ready to go. Mrs. Roosevelt, though eight months pregnant, chose to demonstrate the security of the venture by sailing along with her husband. Her only other companion was a Newfoundland dog named Tiger.

Her courage did little to diminish the number of skeptics. Their doubts seemed confirmed as Halley's comet appeared, blazing in the skies, provoking cries of "Doomsday!" River-dwelling Indians dubbed the strange ship "The Fire Canoe." As the down-river voyage progressed, there were earthquakes, low water, then torrential rains and high water (producing fears of riverbank cave-ins). Mrs.

Roosevelt had to admit that she "lived in a constant fright, unable to sleep or sew or read." But the baby arrived safely and the mother's bravery got the desired press coverage. By mid-January, the *New Orleans* was safely berthed in the city of her name.

That epochal voyage had the effect of opening the West to steamboats; by 1835, there were 684 such vessels navigating the western rivers. It appeared that anyone tough enough to face down the pirates, the snags, the monopolies, the competitive captains, and the shifting channels could participate. The response was so enthusiastic, the variety of boats so extraordinary, that the three decades before the Civil War (the same span of time as the era of canal boats) is often referred to as the "Steamboat Bonanza." In the climactic decade of the 1850s,

Surveyors depicted above were measuring Minnesota's White Bear Lake. More scientific techniques produced better maps for travelers west and south. Opposite: H.S. Tanner's map of Arkansas, below, was published in 1833; August Mitchell's "Texas, Oregon, and California," above, appeared in 1846.

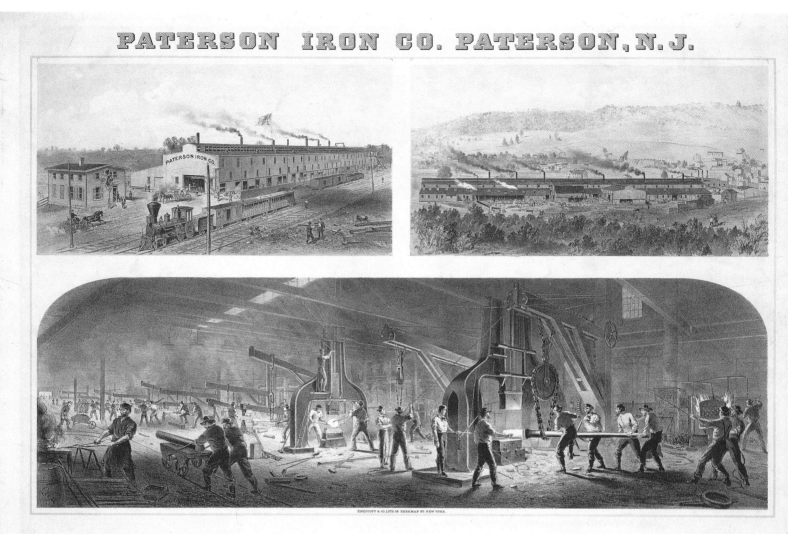

PATERSON IRON CO. PATERSON, N.J.

ENDICOTT & CO. LITH 59 BEEKMAN ST NEW YORK.

STEAMBOAT & RAILROAD FORGINGS.

Essential to less explosive, more sturdy steamboats and locomotives was better casting of iron engine parts. In the promotion piece above, the Paterson Iron Company proclaims its prowess.

steamboat arrivals and departures at the entrepôt of St. Paul, Minnesota, increased from one hundred a year to one thousand.

Before that bonanza of the steamboat years, most of the serious work of opening up the rivers had been carried out by vessels of about the size and tonnage of the 109-ton *Virginia*. This small but capable stern-wheeler had explored the upper Mississippi, reaching the Minnesota River at Fort Snelling in 1823. The year before, a similar steamer had reached Fort Smith on the Arkansas River. Assisted by such supply vessels, ranging up the Missouri, the U.S. Army extended its campaign against the Indians of the West. Travel brochures began to urge curious Americans and would-be settlers

from all the nations of the world to come and see this intriguing, wild and woolly new land.

To carry the new passengers on their way, builders launched such wonders as the extravagantly decorated, twenty-six hundred-ton *Great Republic*, whose main cabin was 275 feet long, with sleeping accommodations for two hundred. No mode of traveling had ever been so splendid. Splendid, yes, but also dangerous; newspapermen referred to the side-wheelers as "floating coffins." Undaunted, indulgent travelers called for bigger and better steamships; Mark Twain remarked that the vessels were "finer than anything on shore." Such a time of opulent splendor (which Henry Adams and other easterners termed decadent) would not be seen again in the history of American maritime transportation.

During the 1850s a recorded 727 steamboats were seen on western rivers (as opposed to seventeen boats in 1817 and sixty-nine in 1820). They moved their passengers and freight less expensively and more swiftly than wagons could ever move them on crushed stone turnpikes or across trussed bridges. By 1860, steamboats were churning the entire twenty-two-hundred-mile distance up the Missouri River to the outpost of Fort Benton, Montana. It appeared that Americans had found the transportation mode by which their continent's interior—or at least the river-accessible parts of it—could be tamed.

River Arteries at the Heart of the Nation

The building of these larger, more powerful boats had been assisted by the decision of engineer-navigator Henry Shreve to import from Philadelphia a number of high-pressure steam engines, the invention of Oliver Evans. With vessels powered by these lighter and more efficient power plants, Captain Shreve had been able to demonstrate his command of the Mississippi and to break the Fulton-Livingston monopoly in 1824. That, as it happened, was also the year of the famous Supreme Court *Gibbons vs. Ogden* decision which prohibited states henceforth from granting monopolies to corporations engaged in interstate commerce. Shreve's highly successful river steamboats, many of them double-decked, were designed with more beam and less draft—shallow enough to be called "dishpans." Though as humble as canal boats, they also got their special job done.

Captain Henry Shreve's greatest contribution to the steamboat era was surely his totally unprecedented vessel named *Heliopolis* (Sun City). This heavy-timbered, twin-hulled craft was equipped at the bow with a cumbrous device, half-crane, half-meathook for ripping out from the bed of the Mississippi the variety of snags and snares that had menaced traffic for all the previous years. By means of his snag boat, the captain did indeed intend to help the sun shine on the newly booming cities of the South.

In fact, as a result of the *Heliopolis*'s successful clearing of some twelve hundred miles of the Mississippi, Shreve's and other steamboats succeeded in stimulating the economies of both North and South. This was done through increasingly sharp management of shipping on the continent's far-reaching rivers, arteries of reliable transportation. Shreve and other merchant-shippers thereby did what they could to unify, at least for a time, the two increasingly opposed sections of the country via one coherent, interior system. Shreveport, Louisiana—the gracious city the Red River runs by before it goes on to form the border of Texas and Oklahoma—is quite justly named after the pioneering captain.

Americans' torrid adventure with steamships seemed to have come and gone in a notably pell-mell manner. That era passed swiftly through initiation and fast growth, cut-throat competition and consolidation and stabilization, then came the years of decline and virtual extinction (mostly caused by inability to compete with railroads). In the first two decades after the Civil War, tonnage on the western rivers declined by more than a third.

During that time, in a certain riverside, steamboat-prosperous city, there were citizens prescient enough to see that the sunny steamboat times might be at an end. The city was St. Louis, the date was 1865, just after the war, and the question was whether now, once again, the rivers would run freely and richly with settlers and freight traffic into the forseeable future. Beware, wrote an editorialist in the *St. Louis Dispatch*; beware lest the city sleep "in fancied security, trusting to its geographical position" at the junction of the Missouri and Mississippi rivers. Should not alternative plans be made for the city if the railroads became the way Americans chose to go?

CHAPTER 3

ROLLING INTO THE

EMPIRE OF

Wagon train after wagon train crossed the rolling plains to the western mountains:
This Currier and Ives print expresses that nationalistic ideal of the nineteenth century.

THE WEST

At the height of the railway-building era in America's far West, between the Civil War and 1900, some six hundred Concord stagecoaches were built by the famous firm of Abbott, Downing in New Hampshire—most of them ordered for service on western wagon roads. One such shipment must have been particularly eye-catching: Thirty magnificently gleaming, red and black stagecoaches had been strapped onto fifteen railroad flatcars; a number of tall-stacked, smoke-belching locomotives had been rounded up to chuff-chuff the flatcars into position. The stagecoaches were outward bound for Leavenworth, Kansas, where they would help the go-for-broke firm of Russell, Majors & Waddell fulfill new mail contracts.

Claiming yet another Rockies peak, General John C. Frémont is portrayed as America's flag-planting hero in the drawings at right and below. Few foresaw then (1842) that railroads—barely emerged from experimental types of propulsion, including horse treadmill and sail, opposite—would conquer the western mountains.

COL. FREMONT
PLANTING THE AMERICAN STANDARD ON THE ROCKY MOUNTAINS.

And so railroads, the technology of the future, assisted stagecoaches, the vehicles of the past. This and other contradictory pictures—shattering the conventional, seamless concept of progress in American transportation history, particularly in the West—keep surfacing. Time and again such twists and lapses appear in the documentary collections of the Library of Congress, signaling that our national obsession with spanning the continent by rails—called the "absorbing passion of our people"—was a passion countered by hang-ups and past love affairs.

Furthermore, the entire enterprise of claiming the West by rail and other advanced means, the adventure of moving into those vast trans-Mississippi expanses, seems (as we turn the pages of the engineering surveys and legislative records) to have been approached with deliberate, gradualist caution, if not actual reluctance. After fur trapper Jedediah Smith's 1824 discovery of South Pass (the critical route through the Rockies), a full generation went

by before the first pioneers climbed up and over it on their way to the Pacific.

This westward hesitancy is, of course, a seeming contradiction of the myth of irrepressible American mobility. It is also at odds with gung-ho legends of impulsive "Pathfinder" John Charles Frémont and other daring blazers of the Santa Fe and Overland trails. But, while less grandiose as a national theme, the fact of gradualism indicates how mighty and majestic the continent loomed in the eyes of nineteenth-century Americans. Trusting at first only in traditional ways of traveling—by shank's mare, by steamboat, by ox-hauled wagons—and slowly inventing other more capital-intensive systems, they moved into their "Empire of the West" with as much respect as courage.

Perhaps the greatest lapse in the ever-forward history of westward transportation (analogous to the time gap between John Fitch's invention of the commercial steamboat and Robert Fulton's *Clermont*) is the strange discontinuity between the triumph of the first

feasible locomotive and the application of that power to the seemingly obvious task of linking the Mississippi with the Pacific by rail. In fact, the first successful, heavy-duty locomotive seen in the Americas—the mighty *Stourbridge Lion*, imported from England in 1829 to help with construction work on the Delaware & Hudson Canal—was abandoned immediately after its trial run. It was too heavy for easily built trestles, its owners felt; so it was allowed to rust and gather weeds outside Carbondale, Pennsylvania, until vandals destroyed it.

A few years later, in 1831, a popular encyclopedia was informing Americans that railroads would "no doubt" soon demonstrate superiority over canals for long-distance traveling. An enthusiastic newspaper in Boston, the *American Traveler*, was simultaneously letting its readers know of the latest developments in railroading, at home and abroad.

Images of railroad locomotives and cars began to appear as decorations on dishes, china, glassware, even whisky bottles. But, despite tremendous hopes and dreams and ballyhoo, three more decades would go by before leaders of this nation could agree how or where to lay tracks into the heart of and across the distances of the West.

The half-continent that lay beyond the Mississippi was undoubtedly awesome and intimidating. But was that intimidation intense enough to explain why by 1857, when more than thirty-five thousand miles of track had been laid in a variety of eastern states (and when some four and a half million of America's thirty million people were living west of the Mississippi), little more than three thousand miles had been put in place in the West?

No, there was something about the railroad—the expense of its construction, the paucity of locomotive manufacturing plants here, among many other things—that caused transportation leaders to cling all the more stubbornly to vehicles of the past. Even as the populace waxed more and more enthusiastic about the possibilities of steam-powered transportation, lawyers and bankers and politicians failed to believe that rails should be trusted or ox power abandoned.

In addition, experts pondered the economic/social issue of who really might own the land, the road on which the rails were to be laid; surely no exclusive relationship should exist between a transportation company and the road on which its vehicles ran. It seemed only proper to Pennsylvania legislators that, on the state-owned line projected between Philadelphia and Columbia in the early 1830s, some twenty companies should be permitted to run trains. Such inefficiencies and confusions nearly strangled the development of railroads in America.

Then there was the matter of whether the steam-powered railroad systems would really work for the transportation of either goods or people. Oh, conservatives said, horse-drawn cars on rails were effective enough; so that was the mode planned for the canal-competitive Baltimore & Ohio Railroad when it was inaugurated in 1828. And there might be some other time-tested ways of moving vehicles along rails—which encouraged a bunch of nostalgic navigators to build and promote a railcar rigged with lofty mast and square sail. This vehicle came to a predictable end. Negative commentators urged all to heed the advice of an "authoritative" book writer in England who had decreed in 1825 that moving people on railroads by steam engines was "extremely improbable."

"Tom Thumb" Loses the Race But Fires the Imagination

These gloomy tidings could not totally restrain the genius of incorrigible tinkerers and self-taught "jacklegs" who carried on in the spirit of Oliver Evans. The names of two Americans stand out, one obscure today, the other well known: Gridley Bryant and Peter Cooper.

It was Bryant, a contractor commissioned to supply the granite for Boston's Bunker Hill

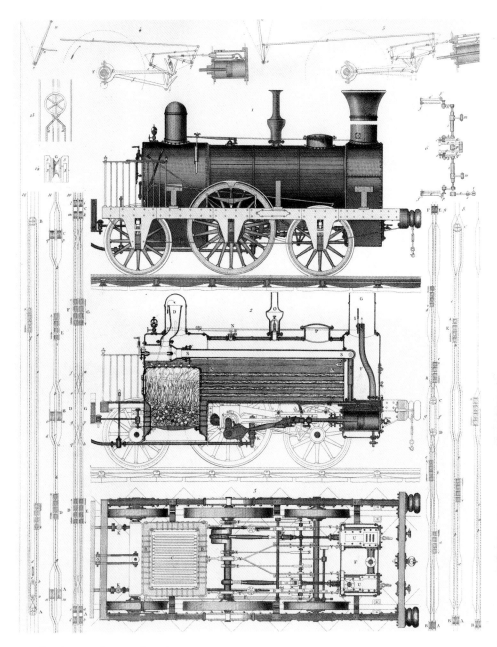

The first locomotive emplaced on an American railroad track: The *Stourbridge Lion,* opposite, was imported from England and given a brief run at Honesdale, Pennsylvania in 1829. Soon everyone was a steam engine expert. J.J. Heck's 1851 *Iconographic Encyclopedia* presented the how-to-build-a-locomotive diagram above.

The "Best Friend," the First Locomotive built in the United States for actual service on a Railroad.

monument, who solved by his innovations many of the problems of switching cars from track to track, controlling them down slopes, and reversing their direction by means of a turntable. After reading of experiments in England, he had begun to ponder the idea of building a railway track from the quarry in Quincy, Massachusetts, to the Neponset River; he had also seen, locally, little tramways on which builders moved materials from one level to another. Could he not do likewise on a larger scale?

His request for a railway charter was nearly turned down in 1826. Daniel Webster, among other worthies, expressed grave doubts about the effect of frost heaves on the rails. But Bryant designed the road bed and the mechanical devices for handling each step of the way so meticulously that the whole process worked without a hitch. Only a single horse was necessary to pull the tremendous load (each car carried sixteen tons). The construction worked so well, in fact, that Bryant's "Granite Line" continued to perform its essential function of delivering stone to harbor profitably for forty years, always by horsepower. The line also succeeded in convincing many of Massachusetts's wiser heads that canals were *not* the way to reach west and hook up with the Erie; rails were the way. Industrialists and politicians even spoke of extending rails beyond the Great Lakes—connecting, as one

said, State Street (Boston's financial district) with the Mississippi. But, of course, it was not quite that simple.

Gridley Bryant died poor and forgotten; fate was kinder to Peter Cooper, whose name lives on in popular history. But it seemed at the time—when Cooper's tiny experimental, anthracite-burning steam engine *Tom Thumb* was raced against a stallion in 1830 along a thirteen-mile stretch of track—that his destiny was also shadowed. For soon after the little engine and its flat car had caught up with and passed the horse (which had charged ahead at first, pulling a wagonful of enthusiasts), a leather drive belt on the steam engine broke. As his machine lost momentum, Peter Cooper struggled to make repairs, but the gallant horse galloped past. The race, which had been organized by stagecoach operators alarmed by rumors of *Tom Thumb's* speed of six miles per hour, went decisively to the horse.

Despite that defeat, news of Peter Cooper's otherwise successful experiments with his engine could not be contained; nor could reports of the *Stourbridge Lion's* success on Pennsylvania's Carbondale and Honesdale Railroad in the previous year. Then, in the spring of 1831, came news of the extraordinary performance of the *Best Friend of Charleston* on the Charleston & Hamburg road in South Carolina: That steam engine and then another one were employed (even after a

Gridley Bryant's innovative railroad at Quincy, Massachusetts demonstrated that weighty loads (like his local granite) could be moved successfully up hill and down along well-constructed tracks. Views of his reconstructed railroad appear opposite. Above: *The Best Friend,* built at the West Point Foundry and shipped to Charleston, South Carolina in 1831, was the first railroad train to keep a regular schedule.

The silhouette of the *DeWitt Clinton,* above, was originally clipped out of black paper with scissors by a keenly observant artist. The photo opposite represents a reenactment of that train's sensational run in 1832.

disastrous explosion) in the regular business of conveying passengers from place to place according to a regular schedule.

Even better news came from New York's Mohawk Valley, scene of the Erie Canal. There, not many months after the *Best Friend of Charleston's* triumph, a locomotive appropriately named *DeWitt Clinton* enjoyed what has been called "the most interesting journey ever undertaken by an early American railroad." It dashed along the seventeen-mile track between Albany and Schenectady at speeds approaching thirty miles an hour, engulfing passengers aboard its three coaches and five flatcars in a thrillingly dangerous deluge of smoke and cinders, giving them all the ride of their lives.

They and the many subsequent observers of the *DeWitt Clinton* at work were so taken by its potential that New York State cast caution aside and began to build railroads to the West. Within but a few years a number of other town and cities across the central part of the state were linked by steam railroad. Eventually these short lines, at the insistence of an enthusiastic train-riding public (which seemed to materialize, fully formed, out of the woodlands), reorganized themselves under one corporate management and took on the name of the New York Central Railroad.

In Massachusetts, too, matters were getting themselves organized, with railway lines from Boston reaching out to the thriving industrial center at Lowell, and with other branches stretching to Worcester and Providence. Eventually (1841) Massachusetts' Western Line reached Albany, the longest and most successful railroad built by a single American corporation.

In Pennsylvania and other striving northern states, networks of short-line railways stretched from town to town, bridging the rivers, threading between the hills. By 1857, as stated above, more than thirty-five thousand miles of track had been laid. The corporately financed railroad, though still shaky (particularly after the excessive speculations and resultant panic of 1837) had become an attractive investment and a dynamic factor in American life. Yet the railroads hesitated at the verge of the Mississippi. If railroad investments in the East had been risky, they might be catastrophic on a larger scale in the West.

Across the Rockies by Foot, Saddle, and Wagon

For all the decades since the Louisiana Purchase of 1803, the American West had essentially belonged to one strange, unsettled

fraternity: the beaver trappers and their Indian colleagues. Much of the West was still under the Spanish or Mexican flag, occupied sparsely by colonists (including religious orders) who had moved into parts of what are today Texas, New Mexico, and California. The somewhat unclear border between the increasingly nationalistic United States and the increasingly threatened Spanish territories was drawn, approximately, along the Red River and the ridge of the continental divide.

"Oregon Country" was an equally vague territory north of California; a border at the 42nd parallel was finally established by the treaty of 1819. This land in the Northwest, where ambitious New Yorkers had established a China-trade port, "Astoria," at the mouth of the Columbia River before the War of 1812, had originally been claimed by Russia and Spain. It was now, in the 1820s and 1830s, under contention by Great Britain and the United States.

Contested and yet unknown, the West was a formidable, two-thousand-mile-wide land of towering mountains and waterless deserts. Even though little steamboats had fought their way up the Missouri (which ran some 3,175 miles from St. Louis to Fort Benton, Montana), very few waterways twisted through the daunt-

ing western mountains. Americans, therefore, would have to find some new type of vehicle for moving overland, of becoming overlanders— some magic wagon powered by superhuman, superanimal means—if they wished to claim the West.

To Native Americans, this land beyond the Mississippi was, of course, no wilderness at all. It was home, the gift of the gods. Preceding and during the time when European-descended Americans set out to claim the Empire of the West, the Indian nations shifted and expanded, responding creatively to new opportunities opened up by horse and rifle. They then suffered terrible devastations from disease, deprivation, and outright slaughter. Ironically, it was certain Indian groups, driven from their homelands by official U.S. actions between 1820 and 1845, who might be considered the first important emigrants to the trans-Mississippi West.

Most notable of these migrations was the infamous removal of the so-called Five Nations (Cherokees, Chickasaws, Choctaws, Creeks, and Seminoles) from their native and legally recognized homes in the Southeast to barren reservations in eastern Oklahoma (where, to double the irony, rich deposits of oil were much later discovered). President

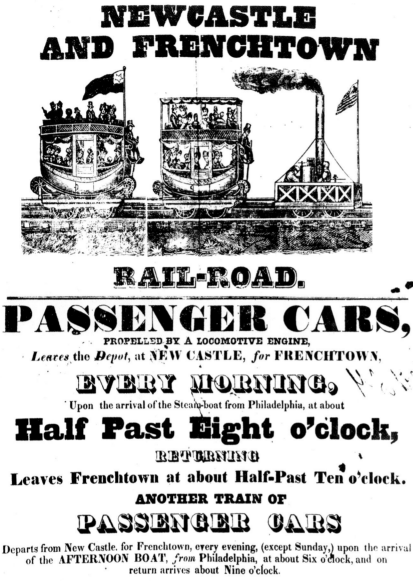

By the early 1830s, ambitious lines in the East wooed travelers with ads like the one above. But in the West frontier families voyaged in prairie schooners—as depicted in William Henry Jackson's view opposite. In the background looms Chimney Rock, a landmark on the trail along the North Platte River from Nebraska to Wyoming.

Andrew Jackson's iron-handed leadership in forcing through Congress the Indian Intercourse Act of 1834—as a result of which four thousand Indians lost their lives while trying to complete the one thousand mile-long "Trail of Tears" across the Mississippi and into the West—cannot be forgotten in this story of how the first Americans moved West.

At that time white expansionists had begun to dream impressively large dreams of how to occupy the continent—canals and rails somehow extending west. Senator Thomas Hart Benton of Missouri imagined a canal that would get around the Rockies by linking the Missouri with the Snake and Columbia rivers. An articulate New York merchant named Asa Whitney, who as a youth had made his fortune in China, devoted the rest of his life to proposing railroad-building schemes to reach the Pacific. But despite all this, the first passages had to be made by foot.

So on foot and horse a group of Congregational missionaries proceeded west and north between April and September of 1836. They were led by a remarkably stalwart pioneer named Marcus Whitman who, the year before (at age thirty-three), had abandoned a country medical practice in New York State to join a colleague in an exploration of the West. Now, accompanied by bride Narcissa and other evangelistic couples, he drove a train of wagons over South Pass, continuing northwest through the Snake and Columbia River valleys to Oregon. Having founded his missionary settlement at Waiilatpu (now Walla Walla, where a national monument has been established to mark the event), he helped bolster America's claim to the Oregon Territory.

More importantly, Marcus and Narcissa Whitman (she being the first white woman to cross the Rockies) showed the way to a new generation of northwest-bound emigrants. As others followed, wagon wheels carved deep ruts into the face of the land; these emblematic wheel tracks took on the proud name of the Oregon Trail.

Then, during the winter of 1840–41, a dozen Missouri families contracted a severe case of "California fever." Naming themselves the Western Emigration Society, they decided to attempt the overland journey to the rumored

green pastures of California, far warmer than misty Oregon. Many were so poor that they wondered if a hundred dollars could be found amongst them all.

With brawny John Bartleson elected train captain and teacher-farmer John Bidwell organizing and chronicling the experience, the families took on the appearance of a serious expedition. Though, as Bidwell wrote later, "No one [of us] knew where to go, not even the captain," they were hopeful, even confident about stories of "rivers flowing from the Great Salt Lake down into California." They succeeded in engaging fur trader Thomas Fitzpatrick as their guide (he had been with Jedediah Smith in the discovery of South Pass). Fitzpatrick agreed to lead Bartleson and Bidwell's company at

least as far as the Hudson Bay Company's trading post at Fort Hall on the Snake River in eastern Idaho; but he knew of no rivers west from there.

The train of ten wagons left the upper Missouri Valley in May 1841. When Fitzpatrick had led them to the crucial turning point east of Fort Hall—where the party might turn north toward Oregon or south in search of those fabled rivers—he said he would only take the northward route. Some of the party heeded the guide's advice but Bartleson and Bidwell still opted for California. Thirty men and one young, babe-in-arms woman, named Mary Kelsey, agreed with their young leaders. Thanks to courage and luck, they made it.

Their route can only be described as epical. It took them around the north end of Great

W.H. JACKSON.

By a variety of vehicles and two- and four-footed power, Americans became "overlanders." Above, William Henry Jackson depicts travelers pushing hand carts; opposite above, sturdy horses get ready for an express mail haul; opposite below, twenty mules are hitched to a heavy shipment of borax, giving that product its brand name, Twenty Mule Team Borax.

Salt Lake, through the natural pass in the Promontory Mountain Range, then south to a second pass through the jagged black peaks of the Pilot Range along today's Utah-Nevada border. From there the Bartleson-Bidwell party's train of ten wagons crossed Utah. Unwittingly, they pioneered the route to Sacramento that would become the path of both the Pony Express and the Pacific Railroad.

The route was rugged; the wagons had to be abandoned and the group reorganized as a pack train while they struggled against star-

vation by living off the land. But eventually (on September 23, well before the onslaught of winter) they reached the headwaters of the seemingly miraculous Humboldt River in the Ruby Mountains, south of present-day Elko, Nevada. This river valley, though not leading to the sea and though characterized by awesome gorges (as railroad surveyors would find later), was the only natural route across northern Nevada.

John Bidwell turned out to be as good a journalist as he was a pack-train organizer;

74

his enthusiastic diary, printed in 1842, encouraged others to travel toward the rainbow of the West. Responding to his call and to the news of the Whitmans' settlement, hundreds and thousands of ready-to-go Americans loaded their goods into canvas-topped wagons—"prairie schooners"—and took to the trail. They live in the pages of history as the "Great Migration of 1843."

Some of these emigrants were as fortunate as the Bartleson-Bidwell party, often finding their own way through the mountain passes, winching their wagons up over the bluffs, contending with hostile Indians and horrendous storms. Others were far less fortunate—most notably the members of the Donner party of 1847, seven of whom survived by countenancing cannibalism while stranded in the mountains.

Despite such disasters, the numbers of arrivals in the West kept mounting. Some fourteen hundred pilgrims passed successfully along the Oregon Trail in 1844. During the next year nearly five thousand people in five companies reached the northwestern territory. Then in 1846, while an estimated 1,350 emigrants were on the Trail, the British, realizing that Americans had successfully made their case, abandoned claims to Oregon.

Unfortunately, the Whitmans were unable to enjoy for long their success as colonizers.

graphical Engineers had reconnoitered the Oregon Trail on two separate expeditions. Although no one knew exactly what his official mission was, he was never challenged, for he was, among other things, the son-in-law of Missouri's Senator Thomas Hart Benton. The officer's name was John Charles Frémont; as brilliant in mathematics as dashing in appearance, he would become in the minds and hearts of many the spirit of the Western Empire.

Senator Benton's initial anger on learning of his daughter's elopement with and marriage to this illegitimate, ambitious Charleston math

Frank Leslie's Illustrated Newspaper took the lead in covering travel out West. An illustration at right from that journal shows passengers changing from mail coach to "celebrity wagon." Above, conveyors of the all-important U.S. mail attempt a river crossing at night.

In 1847, when the Cayuse tribe contracted measles from white immigrants and died in great numbers, a band of braves took matters into their own hands. Breaking into the mission at Walla Walla, they massacred Marcus, Narcissa, and ten others.

Heroes of the Expanding West

Shortly before the deaths of the Whitmans, a young officer in the army's Corps of Topo-

teacher dissipated as he foresaw advantages in having a surveyor and rover in the family. Frémont had a way of returning from a voyage with the right kind of information. Perhaps the young officer could assist Benton's own plans of opening up the West.

At the conclusion of his 1842 expedition, Frémont declined to obey army orders that he return immediately to headquarters. Instead, guided by Thomas Fitzpatrick and Kit Carson, and counting on Senator Benton for protection, he went off on a voyage of his own to determine if there really were rivers flowing out of Great Salt Lake to the Pacific. Not discouraged by the negative finding, and barely surviving an ill-advised crossing of the snow-heaped Sierra Nevada at Carson Pass, Frémont made his way to Sutter's Fort near Sacramento (where gold would soon be discovered) and rode home via the southern California route to Colorado.

The reports of that harrowing journey and his earlier trip to the South Pass were replete with details on how he hoisted a flag on Frémont Peak in the Wyoming Rockies, crossed Great Salt Lake on a raft, battled snowdrifts in the Sierras and skirmished with Indians in the Mojave Desert. These adventures were written up with the aid of Jessie Frémont, as talented a promoter as she was devoted a wife.

Her colorful accounts, entitled *Report of the Exploring Expedition to the Rocky Mountains in the Year 1842 and to Oregon and North California in the Years 1843-44*, gave splendid publicity to the new American hero. But they were also quite accurate, enormously helpful, geographical descriptions of western routes. Attracted by them, a youthful generation redoubled its efforts to find the way West. Frémont soon headed to California again, encouraged by his father-in-law toward even more daring acts. Specifically, he was interested in seeing what might be done to liberate the region from its Spanish and Mexican masters.

The other inspiring figure to demonstrate the accessibility of the West (if one didn't mind a few hardships along the trail) was the Mormon leader, Brigham Young. Having inherited the prophet's mantle from murdered founder Joseph Smith, Brigham Young sought to strengthen and direct the growing population of Mormons at their new site on the east bank of the Mississippi in Illinois (Nauvoo). In 1845, hearing of trails opening toward the West, he contemplated solving the problem of rising hatred among the Mormons' neighbors by leading his people to an undisclosed, unknown destination in the formerly Spanish, then Mexican, lands across the river.

The epic voyage of the Mormon thousands to Salt Lake City, begun in the late winter of 1846 and completed in July 1847, must be viewed as a special chapter in the history of Americans moving west. The story is replete with wonders and apparent miracles, such as the seagulls that arrived barely in time to destroy the crop-devouring locusts. But the survival and endurance of so many thousands (some of whom hauled their own two-wheeled carts by hand) is surely the most impressive feature of the Mormons' astonishing venture. With the successful completion of their fifteen hundred-mile trek, Brigham Young and his multitudinous followers demonstrated that at least one type of American was capable of meeting the challenges and grasping the opportunities of the vast western landscape.

Indeed, Americans of several persuasions seemed ready to demonstrate a new readiness for mountains and deserts. These were certainly not drifters; in the language of their day, they had become "hard-twisted pioneers." Adventurer J. C. Frémont and prophet Brigham Young, larger-than-life heroes, led the way, but it was the bulk of nameless pioneers themselves who, given increasing economic incentives, made this their land (or became the land's, as Robert Frost might say). Theirs was the awful task of crossing the continent by foot; theirs the glory of endowing subsequent Americans with an inclination to move.

Gold and Silver in the West

The trail from Independence, Missouri, to Santa Fe stretched for eight hundred miles, eight hundred miles of Indian-contested territory, cactus-spotted deserts, red-rocked mountains. It had been described as "The Great American Desert" in the vivid report of Major Stephen H. Long in 1820. Risking those distances, and out to trade for furs among the Comanches in the decisive year of 1821, Captain William Beckworth and a handful of companions rode south of the border marking the Spanish territories. Suddenly, to their dismay, they saw clouds of dust rising in the distance, apparently an armed band.

Beckworth's fears eased slightly when the approaching strangers turned out to be friendly Mexican soldiers, eager to tell him of their nation's just-declared independence. Urged on to the provincial capital of Santa Fe, the captain-turned-merchant hoped he might find some purchasers for his trade goods. His hopes were swiftly and amply rewarded. Returning home with handsome profits (having chosen a route over Raton Pass which later came to be known as the Mountain Branch of the Santa Fe Trail), Beckworth sparked a blaze of commercial expectation on the frontier.

The importance of the Santa Fe Trail—which, Congress thought, deserved precise surveying by means of a $30,000 grant—lay in the silver and gold with which Mexicans could pay for American goods. Beaver pelts from western streams were, to be sure, a hefty part of the vigorous trade that sprang up between Santa Fe and Independence; but the Mexicans' gold and silver coins were what made the whole relationship gleam with a special brightness. Dry goods and hardware from the northeast and cotton from the southeast constituted the exchange from the American side. And so the wagons rumbled heavily out from Missouri and rolled richly back; the Santa Fe Trail became as busy a route for commercial development as the Oregon Trail was for the people's emigration.

Then gold, gold, and more gold became the dominant factor in the movement of people toward California. Discovered at Sutter's Mill on the American River in 1848—soon after the Mormons had established themselves at Salt Lake City and the Santa Fe Trail had become a major route west—the gold of California drew additional thousands west, exercising the power of a polar magnet. By clipper ships around Cape Horn or by steamer to Central America (and, for some, across Nicaragua on a paved road built by perspicacious Cornelius Vanderbilt), then into San Francisco Bay by sail or steam the immigrants streamed. Others made the attempt by land. By 1857, a dozen years before the continent was spanned by rails, more than 165,000 men, women, and children had made that great trek—a journey that to an earlier generation had seemed nearly impossible, a challenge for saints and heroes exclusively. Americans had become overlanders.

Schooners and High Plains Freighters

Having been given romantic heroes and economic incentives, westward pioneers now required increasingly dependable vehicles to move them in even greater numbers. The old term "prairie schooner" was actually a romantic coverall for a variety of simple, canvas-topped wagons. Some of these descended directly from the Conestogas, others were but crude farm wagons. They tended to be less capacious than the heavy carriers of the high-plains freighters, whose sixteen-foot carriage beds could carry five tons and more. But, light or heavy, the pioneers' wagons shared the common characteristic of creakiness; the wood-bearing axles had to be heavily greased every day (not until 1845 were iron axles introduced). They also shared slowness—plus a certain grace.

When Samuel Bowles, editor of the *Republican* of Springfield, Massachusetts, toured the West during this pre-railroad era, he wrote eloquently of the wagon trains (some of which were a third of a mile long. "They remind one," he wrote, "of the caravans described in the Bible and other Eastern books." Out northwestward along the shallows of the North Platte River they would roll on their way to the South Pass and the Oregon Trail or out southwestward along the Arkansas River on their way to Bent's Fort and the Santa Fe Trail. Emigrants who could not afford to organize a wagon and team often walked along, serving as driver's or cook's helpers.

Credit for hauling the wagons west—for which the wagon master's early morning call was, "Stretch out! Stretch out!"—must also go to the expendable animals who did the stretching. When horses were put to harness, they pulled on command until thirst and hunger and exhaustion stopped them in their tracks. Then, as was the case with the Bartleson party, the animals' throats were slit and their meat (such as it was) consumed. The huge, "Conestoga" horses of the eastern teamsters proved not quite adequate for the West because they required good grain for fodder and time for recuperation.

Mules, though more expensive and less lovable than horses, lived longer lives, ate

about a third less food, and walked with surer feet on mountain passes. Best worker of all, however, was the ox; though these mighty pullers were dreadfully slow (one or two miles per hour), they had the great virtue of being able to find fodder for themselves in the high plains during the winter months. Although their hooves occasionally proved vulnerable to long hauls over rocky surfaces, inventive teamsters found a way to apply iron shoes (the ox was put upside down in a ditch, helplessly submitting to the process).

The extraordinary men who managed these beasts also deserve remembrance for their contributions. These were the "bullwhackers" who so patiently yet forcefully managed the oxen; the "muleskinners" who could get cooperation from a train of twenty or thirty balky

mules; the wagon masters who bore ultimate responsibility for the endless trains, which included protecting them tactically against the Indian attacks. Earning the lordly sum of $100 a month for their labors in the early days of this strenuous business (when a "dollar a day" was "a good man's pay"), wagon masters commanded $150 a month by 1860.

The western landscape beckoned even more seductively after American expansionists had managed a war with Mexico. By the Treaty of Guadalupe Hidalgo (1848), California and Texas and the Utah and New Mexico Territories were legally added to the United States. But the technology that hauled emigrants and goods across vast distances continued to move on four feet, slowly. Not many improvements could be made—though rope ferries did become more

Through newly settled communities of the West trooped endless pack trains of surefooted horses, for this was the only way to get supplies up and over the mountains. A photographer sighted this pack train above in Kooskia, Idaho.

In a land without bridges, wide rivers posed a constant problem. Here, a coach is halted on the bank of New Mexico's Pecos River, and mailmen haul sacks to the other side via a continuous line.

efficient, capable in some heavy-traffic locations of carrying 225 wagons a day cross-river. One critic remarked that no nation could exist as merely a number of states and territories sprawled on either side of a two-thousand-mile desert, joined by animal power, wagons, and ferries. Where was the presidential leadership? The unfortunate legacy of early turnpike building may have dictated that the federal government should take no role in highway (or railway) building—but did that mean that no one in Washington could help develop a nationwide transportation system?

Tensions between North and South, rather than being eased by westward expansions and possibilities, were exacerbated by them. In which

territories would slavery rule; in which would it be banned? Since cotton was undeniably king throughout the land—in the manufacturing North as well as in the plantations of the South—the Compromise of 1850 (by which the Utah and New Mexico Territories could admit slavery) tended to favor Southern interests even more than had the Compromise of 1830 (by which slavery was permitted in Missouri).

Meanwhile, a notable rivalry had developed between two of America's transportation centers: St. Louis, Missouri, at the junction of the Mississippi and Missouri Rivers, and Chicago, Illinois, on the shores of Lake Michigan (and thus, in transportation terms, the "stepchild of the Erie Canal"). Chicago financiers succeeded in linking their city to the west-facing Missouri town of St. Joseph (via Hannibal) by rail in 1854. The St. Louis promoters—whose patron saint, Senator Benton, had been defeated in 1854 but who were still desperate not to be left behind—succeeded in building the "Pacific Railroad" (later known as the Missouri Pacific) to Independence and Kansas City in 1859.

Thus, in the decade before the Civil War, American railways were finally looking creatively toward the West; animal power might soon be replaced. But the politicians and railroad planners squabbled as much as they planned; essentially, they were stalled. While that embarrassment endured, the spanning of the West by horse, mule, and ox power reached a climax.

America's Speediest Wagon— the Concord Coach

In England, the famous *stagecoach*—in which fair ladies were wont to travel, fearing that highwaymen men might interrupt them and the royal mail's delivery—had been a feature of the cultural scene all through the eighteenth and early nineteenth centuries. But those jouncing coaches had been doomed by the English railroads in the 1840s. Similarly, in the eastern United States, stagecoaches had been the best and fastest way of traveling ever since their introduction after the Revolution. But soon after easterners caught "railroad fever," stagecoaches became a fondly remembered anachronism.

In the West, however, the stagecoach prospered as the century advanced. The first version of a stagecoach had reached Wheeling in August of 1817 via the National Road; its slightly evolved grandchild advanced to the Mississippi Valley ten years later. Gradually, increasingly sophisticated coaches worked their way west. In May 1849, an organization calling itself the "Pioneer Line" advertised in St. Louis newspapers that its coaches could take passengers to the diggings in California (a distance of twenty-five hundred miles) within seventy days. And the price for that blinding-fast journey was a mere $200.

The claim was fraudulent. After a few weeks of dusty torture on trails over mountain and desert, the passengers gratefully turned back; the company failed. But the dream remained: Somehow Americans must make their way west more swiftly and more securely than by the three-month journey required in the fastest clippers around the Horn. Calling them all the more urgently to the trans-Mississippi territories were new agricultural inventions (specifically the McCormick reaper of 1834) which lured a future generation of homesteaders who could use machines to plant and reap extraordinary prairie harvests.

Hope for faster transportation rose when the so-called Concord coach, having proved itself in the East, made its first appearance on the San Francisco docks (via the Cape) in June 1850. If the challenge of speeding through the West by horse and carriage was to be met, no one doubted that it would be with the aid these highly specialized vehicles, called the "queen of coaches," priced at $1,500 each.

They were the creation of a mechanical genius named J. Stephen Abbott, who had been in partnership with Lewis Downing, a coach manufacturer since 1826. Together, in Concord, New Hampshire, they devised a coach body and springing system that appeared in integrated form on the roads about 1835; superior engineering made their product world-famous by mid-century. Unlike the rather heavy, iron-bound English coaches, the New Hampshire vehicles were made of the lightest wood, weighing a mere twenty-five hundred pounds. An ovoid shape gave the bodies sufficient strength to withstand the buffeting; the bodies were suspended not on steel springs but on leather straps from corner posts.

They were lofty, highly varnished conveyances—whose underbodies glowed bright red. Romantic landscapes or portraits of actresses decorated the side panels (as opposed to the coaches of colonial days, whose panels had generally pictured Franklin). The rear wheels measured five feet high, the front wheels three feet, ten inches high. This differential helped balance the drive and the steering; it also gave the whole creation what might today be called a "go-fast" look. The wheels, like the body, were examples of superb, hand-tooled joinery, needing no bolts or screws to hold them together.

For westerners at mid-century this meant that a dependable, swift, even glamorous vehicle had been provided, a joy to travel in. Operating the fast-running team with six pairs of loosely held reins was, in one commentator's words, "like playing Bach on a run-away organ." Passengers responded to the Concord coach and its exalted reinsmen with a loyalty that is quite correctly portrayed in pictures of the day and films of later years. The heart of the West forever rides the stagecoach.

With swelling numbers of newly arrived Californians demanding assistance from Congress in establishing a rapid-delivery mail and passenger route, a bill for such service was finally passed in 1856—the assumption being that Concord coaches would be employed. Two routes were projected: one through South Pass (for the construction of which $300,000 was allowed); the other from San Antonio through El Paso to San Diego ($200,000). Washington, in the grip of Southern senators, favored the latter route, pointing out that it would be snow-free for more months of the year. San Franciscans howled in outrage: How could they be omitted from the main route? Transportation moguls in St. Louis and Chicago joined the chorus, arguing that the more northerly route was shorter, therefore faster.

At last, in 1858, a kind of compromise was agreed upon whereby the stagecoaches would wander from the railhead near St. Louis down to El Paso; from there along to Tucson and San Antonio, eventually up to San Francisco. It was a 2,758-mile, "oxbow" route through the southwest that showed, among other things, how much America still had to learn about making transportation efficient. Some $600,000 a year was called for by way of subsidy.

To serve the line, more than one thousand horses were rounded up at a cost exceeding $1,000,000—as well as eight hundred sets of harnesses, five hundred vehicles (about half of which were Concord coaches, the others support wagons), and eight hundred employees positioned along the way at two hundred way stations and relay points. The fare between St. Louis and San Francisco was $200;

half that for the same route eastward; since everyone wanted to go West, those travelers would have to support the enterprise. The passage was supposed to take only twenty-five days.

When the first stagecoach arrived on time (in twenty-three days, twenty-three and a half hours from St. Louis, an average rate of something less than five miles an hour), the event was so important to the nation that the line's founder, David Butterfield, telegraphed the news to President Buchanan. The president replied, "I congratulate you upon the result. It is a glorious triumph for civilization and the Union. Settlements will follow the course of the road, and the East and West will be bound together by a chain of living Americans which can never be broken."

Buchanan's forecast was accurate enough, but misplaced. The ridiculousness of such a lengthy route was soon realized; some drivers got themselves and their passengers hopelessly lost, to everyone's embarrassment and danger. Attacks by roving Indians began to intensify, giving the lie to claims that agreements had been made with all the affected native groups. And when new gold discoveries were made in Colorado, the advantages of a central route—the pathway through South Pass which had been taken so many years before by the Bartleson-Bidwell party—became clear enough for all to see. Though improved by new links and shortcuts, this route (known as the Central Overland Route) was the one to be followed by stagecoaches in all the years through the 1870s, even after the railroads had finally asserted their superiority as long-distance carriers.

It was also along this Central Overland Route that the Pony Express flourished for little more than one fabulous year, 1860. The idea of such a service had been developing in California for two years. State leaders considered it insulting that, though Butterfield's original oxbow route had been dependable enough, it delivered mail semiweekly, not daily; a piece of mail required between eighteen and twenty-four days to reach San Francisco from St. Louis.

Popular literature abounds with descriptions of how the Pony Express organized its successful run, with a band of frontier-toughened

The route of the Pony Express blazes across the illustrated map at left below—virtually two thousand miles from the Missouri River terminus to San Francisco. In the unlikely scene at left above, an expressman doffs his hat to telegraph workers whose wires will end his rides.

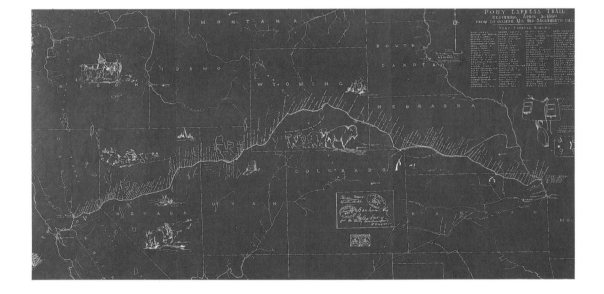

riders (none under eighteen in age or over 120 pounds in weight) galloping the mail along the ten-mile segments of the nearly two thousand-mile system in eight days. Literature also sparkles with descriptions of successors of Butterfield's Overland Stage Line—most notably, Wells Fargo & Co.—and of the vast sums invested by private corporations and public bureaus in these Rockies-leaping lines. But the absurdly brief, one-year life of the Pony Express (until it was ended by the telegraph)

and the horrendous debts and governmental scandals of the mail and freighting companies receive scant attention. Wells Fargo (which later became American Express) was one of the few well-managed stagecoach operations, deriving most of its revenues from well-armed deliveries of silver shipments to eastern banks after exploitation of Nevada's Comstock Lode began in 1859.

The effect of these innovative transportation and communications systems was nearly

what President Buchanan had predicted: Settlements followed the establishment of westward routes, and the nation became increasingly united, East and West—even as the South continued to pursue its dangerously separate course.

All the more astonishing is that by 1870 (when these horse-powered, pre-rail systems reached their peak and the total population numbered about forty million), there had developed a "floating population" of hundreds of thousands in the United States. These floaters were people on the move, the road their home, "passing-through" their song. A new way of being, of being American, had come to pass.

The Golden Spike

"We have got done praying. The spike is about to be presented." With these words, a telegraph operator reported the status of ceremonies to hail the meeting of rails from East and West. His somewhat wry message meant that the official honorifics were nearly over. Then, with the driving of a symbolic "golden spike" to hold down the last rail, the country was finally nailed together.

The story of what lay behind that dramatic celebration of May 10, 1869—as well as behind the nation's final awakening from the three-decades-long sleep during which little had been done to cross the Mississippi into the West by railroad—can best be derived from political and economic analysis, not from technological annals. For the question remains: Why did Americans keep setting up roadblocks to prevent their rolling west? Our business interests, our brand of politics provided both the cause for the delay and the cure.

For much of that lost time, the urge to cross the country by rails had been dissipated in political maneuverings between Southern and Northern politicians. Our capitalists had been enslaved by King Cotton and entranced by new industries. The thought rarely occurred that transportation might also be an industry. It was only when Abraham Lincoln assumed power in the White House and when the South seceded from the Union that the shorter, more effective route could be selected; Lincoln's Pacific Railway Act of July 1, 1862, set up the mechanism for the final action, getting America on board the railroads.

That Act created the Union Pacific Railroad, an agency authorized to construct a railroad westward from Council Bluffs, Iowa (later moved to Omaha, Nebraska). It also authorized the previously existing Central Pacific Railroad Company to construct a road eastward from Sacramento—along a route that had been surveyed by the indefatigable and inspired railroad promoter, Theodore D. Judah.

While Judah's discovery of the route over Little Truckee Pass represented a triumph over the railroad-resistant topography of the Sierra Nevada range, it was an even greater triumph over the pro-South philosophy of former Secretary of War, Jefferson Davis. Under Davis's direction in 1853–54, a series of expensive investigations had been conducted, resulting in the twelve-volume work entitled *Exploration and Surveys, Railroad Route Mississippi River to the Pacific Ocean*, visible today in all its cartographic beauty and convoluted reasoning in the Library of Congress.

In sum, the surveys recommended—supposedly for reasons of construction cost—that a southern route be followed, a route that would take advantage of the recently executed Gadsden Purchase (which gave the United States key lands south of New Mexico's Gila River). But in fact Davis's recommendation, which called for the westward line to begin in Memphis and sweep down through Texas then back up to Los Angeles, was little more than an updated version of the excessively lengthy ox bow route of the freighters.

Work on the Central Pacific began immediately, on October 26, 1863, with the laying of

Needed for completion of a mountain-crossing rail system: enough picks and shovels to dig passes through the Rockies like "Bloomer Cut" at Auburn, California, on the Central Pacific Route, left. Heavy locomotives for long hauls on steep grades were also needed. The patriotically decorated A.J. Johnson engine opposite was built at Cleveland in 1874.

Artists for *Leslie's Weekly* showed the difficulties of carving railbed for the Union Pacific into the steep side of Webster Canyon, Utah, above. That line finally reached Promontory Point on the other side of Salt Lake City and joined with the Central Pacific on May 10, 1869. Celebrations of the two lines' linking soon became artistic cliches, opposite.

the first rail. But the issue of when work might begin on the Union Pacific still hung in the air. Here we see nineteenth-century Americans pulled this way and that by the contradictions and indecisions of their day. Finally, two years after it had been legislated (and after lengthy delays as Missouri Valley towns fought over which would be the official departure terminal), track-laying began at Omaha in 1865.

For those financiers who now hoped that the transcontinental railroads might be their way to riches, the stalled year of 1864 had been the perfect time to get through Congress a new Railroad Act which would give them their best-possible deal. While Lincoln's first Act had called for the government to pay off

investors with land grants—the first time that this had been done in American history—those grants were now doubled, and the rights to coal, iron, and timber on those lands were increased. The corporations' bonds were now set up in the form of a first mortgage on the road, with the United States holding the second mortgage (the reverse of the original arrangement). Furthermore, the contractors for the railroads were now much more handsomely rewarded for each mile of work completed; the fee of $16,000 per mile was increased, in some cases to $32,000 and in other cases (where the work was more arduous) to $48,000. Investors' money rolled in from eastern capitalists, particularly those in Boston and New York.

By this program, all parties received more money for laying the rails faster. It was probably that incentive, not noble commitment to national interest, that finally broke the jam at Omaha: The easterners had no intention of letting the western track-layers get all the money. Another cause for delay seemed to have been eliminated when President Lincoln made the decision *not* to adhere to the four-foot, eight-inch measurement between rails which had become the standard in the East. Instead he nodded to the West, where a more rational five-foot gauge prevailed, decreeing that should be the standard. But then Congress, perceiving that this was not a technological but a regional political matter (with the votes and

the money in the Northeast), outflanked the President and restored the shorter measurement as the all-American gauge.

Yet how would America summon the labor force to do the actual digging, the blasting, the rail-laying? For work on the Union Pacific, the answer lay in the astonishing number of wagon trains that were then rolling west, so numerous in this postwar period that five thousand teams were seen crossing the plains in each month of 1865. The wagons were jammed both with Confederate veterans and liberated slaves, all desperate for work, as well as with European immigrants. In Europe (including Ireland), foresighted ship lines had already established agencies that promised work to anyone willing to heave a pickax.

PANORAMIC VIEW OF MAUCH CHUNK, PA · ᴬᴺᴰ VICINITY

Americans paid a price for pell-mell construction of rails across the nation: despoiled land in many areas. Mauch Chunk, in Pennsylvania's anthracite-rich Lehigh Valley, seen in the panorama above, is an oft-cited example. Mightier timber saws—like those advertised opposite—contributed to the land abuse.

For California's Central Pacific, tycoon Charles Crocker had the shrewd idea of employing Chinese laborers. Although others initially opposed this radical suggestion, they were ultimately won over by the excellence of the work done by early Chinese workers and by the cheapness of the pay ($30 in gold, but no board, whereas Caucasians were paid the same in cash, with an extra allowance for board). These remarkable Asian workmen are best remembered in vivid newspaper sketches, showing them hacking away at passages through the Sierra Nevada, clinging roped to the rock face, lowering the cut rock down in wicker baskets.

The Chinese also played a significant part in the introduction of nitroglycerine to the construction of the Central Pacific. Essential to the completion of the work on time, nitroglycerine was far more powerful than the blasting powder previously used. An English chemist named James Howden had taken on the dangerous assignment of delivering the excitable mixture to contractors. But Howden, who was assisted in his work by Chinese laborers, soon fell victim to stress and drink. Undeterred by his death and having learned how to make the stuff, the Chinese assistants carried on. No one knows how many of them lost their lives because of their unstable product.

Another innovation essential to on-time crossing of the Sierra Nevada was the humble snowshed. Until Crocker and the other directors of the Central Pacific agreed on the necessity for these structures, many work crews had been engulfed by monstrous snowstorms in mountains where the Donner party and other pioneers had perished. "No one can face these storms when they are in earnest," concluded one discouraged engineer.

So, against the winter of 1869 (the final winter of work), massive timber sheds were built over the track beds; their ruggedness was matched only by their nearly incredible length. By the end of that fall, some sixty-five million feet of timber and nine hundred tons of bolts and spikes had been used. As Arthur Brown, superintendent of buildings and bridges, reported, "The total length of sheds and galleries when finished was about 37 miles, at a cost of over $2 million."

In the East, contractors also found new and uniquely American ways to speed the work. Legend still recalls the "Hell on Wheels" prefabricated towns that the hard-driving Casement brothers concocted to take workers from one location to another. These worker communities, it must be noted, were more remarkable for their industrial efficacy than for their Christian virtues: No-longer-ladies called "soiled doves" or "femmes du pave" were a regular part of the scene, as were epic brawls and careless murders.

Yet the most remarkable aspect of the work system that evolved under the whip-wielding Casement brothers on the Union Pacific was belt-line production, which echoed Eli Whitney's systems for arms manufacturing in Connecticut. Thanks to this mass production and the synchronized ways in which crews of twelve men were drilled to pick up a rail and carry it into place, the pace of rail laid increased from but one mile per day in 1865 to six or seven miles in 1869—with four rails put in place each minute.

Sped along by human sweat and death, production efficiencies, and natural competitiveness, even while harassed by Indians, weather, and the difficulty of transporting necessary materials to the work site (material for the Cen-

tral Pacific, including locomotives, had to be shipped around Cape Horn), the two lines gradually approached each other from respective sides of the Rockies. But such were the remaining inefficiencies in the business of American railroading that no one seemed capable of determining precisely where the lines should meet. Finally it was President U. S. Grant who forced a decision upon the feuding executives. Grumpily they agreed: The two lines would meet at Promontory Point, Utah, on the north shore of Great Salt Lake.

As might be expected in nineteenth-century America, the final surge toward the completion point called for a massive wager: The Central Pacific boasted that its men could lay ten miles of track in one day. Selecting a notably flat stretch of land, the crews moved out to the workplace as the sun rose—and won the bet by laying ten miles and two hundred feet of rails (weighing more than two million pounds) by sundown at 7 P.M.

Americans from coast to coast recognized this Mississippi-to-Pacific achievement for what it was, something uniquely theirs, something that grew out of their historic, national experience and that looked forward to their national destiny. Engraved on the golden spike,

which was driven into place after a few official fumbles of the hammer once the praying had stopped, were these words:

> May God continue the unity of our country
> as this railroad unites the two great oceans
> of the world.

Editor Samuel Bowles thought it necessary to add a few more words about the significance of the joining of the Pacific railroads. On his mind were the global consequences of the golden spike, but something more. Throughout the effort to extend rails from the Mississippi to the Pacific, politicians and editorialists had imagined gaining access thereby to the riches of the Orient (an access actually won by the British Empire with the Suez Canal, completed in the same year of 1869). But now Samuel Bowles was thinking, additionally, of the consequences to the American spirit. He wrote this of the unification by railroad: "It is ... the unrolling of a new map, a revelation of a new empire, the creation of a new civilization." Here, indeed, was a civilization that would roll on wheels, conditioned no longer by the land but by the act of passing through it.

CHAPTER 4

DESIGNING THE MOBILE SOCIETY

The cover of *Motor* magazine invited Americans to attend the Annual Auto Show of 1933 and to take part in a new era of travel—not by mass-service rail but by individual cars.

All hesitation about railroading westward seemed eliminated by the events of 1869 at Promontory Point, Utah. Hammer blows on commemorative spikes transmitted the prideful message that the world's two hemispheres had been joined by rail in the western United States. Americans responded with flag-waving zeal and the vigor of a young giant: Our swift completion of coast-to-coast railroad lines required but a few years, constituting what historians have termed a "national obsession."

In the frontier-minded heart of the country, this new era truly began in 1874 with the building of a mighty, three-arched railroad bridge across the Mississippi River

MOTOR

ANNUAL SHOW NUMBER
JANUARY · ONE DOLLAR

General Eads's three-arched bridge at St. Louis, shown under construction above and completed opposite, took railroads across the Mississippi to the West and to their heyday at the end of the nineteenth century. Note the obsolescent steamboat at the foot of the unfinished bridge.

at St. Louis, engineered by the builder of Civil War ironclads, James Buchanan Eads. In the awakened East, 1874 saw a $20 million railroad tunnel pierce through Massachusetts' Berkshire Hills, allowing the Boston & Albany to take the shortest possible route over the Hudson River toward the Great Lakes, across the expansive plains, toward the Orient.

A few years earlier, in 1870, easterners had been enabled for the first time to ride without shifting trains from New York through New Jersey and Philadelphia to the nation's capital. The old pattern of short, locally dominant lines was coming to an end. Even George Stevens's exploitative, monopolistic Camden-Amboy Railroad, which had succeeded for years in charging whatever it wanted for the New York–Philadelphia trip, was now linked up cooperatively with other lines.

Fearing the collapse of their hold on freight and passenger systems, conservative local interests had struck back against the new modes whenever and wherever they could: West of Chicago, the Rock Island Line's attempts to cross the Mississippi in the late 1860s were frustrated by steamboat owners who brought

suit against the constitutionality of any river-restricting bridge. The steamboats lost their case only when a brilliant lawyer named Abraham Lincoln (Who ever dreamed he would be President?) was hired to champion the rights of interstate passage. Later the Rock Island Railroad was imperiled by the destruction of its bridge by a suspicious fire. But when a successful cross-Missouri bridge was built at Council Bluffs, Iowa, in 1870, Americans could finally travel by train, unimpeded, from the Atlantic to the Pacific.

It was not until the building of the Eads Bridge at St. Louis, however, that railroads west gained a credible symbol. The bridge stands solid today against the wiles of our mightiest river, demonstrating that the nation finally had the technological capability, the political cohesiveness, and the capitalistic potential to span its distances. The bridge's two stone piers, "miraculously" established in midstream and founded on bedrock, represented America's determination to let neither rivers nor mountains nor special interests interfere with its travel plans. So did Massachusetts' victory over the Berkshires, the Hoosac Tunnel,

which, at four and three fourths miles in length (and 195 lives lost in construction) proclaimed itself the longest underground structure in the world, even if not quite the main line to China.

These engineering marvels were attention-getting parts of what must have seemed the greatest physical accomplishment one nation might ever aspire to: In the fifty years between 1870 and 1920, Americans constructed the world's largest railway system, with 114,000 miles of track added to what had already existed. By 1876 passengers could speed from New York to San Francisco in eighty-three hours, twenty-seven minutes; by 1893 the number of lines stretching to the Pacific had increased from one to five. Besides the Union Pacific, these included James J. Hill's very own Great Northern (built without federal assistance), the Northern and the Southern Pacific lines, and the Atcheson, Topeka & Santa Fe. Although the forging of these rich men's rail empires struck some commentators as an indulgent "orgy," the resultant railroads constituted a huge national asset, a unique accomplishment for that time in world history.

Yet even that would be surpassed. What the grandchildren of those early transportation leaders accomplished in the course of the *next* fifty years, between 1920 and 1970, was even more imperial. Encyclopedists are wont to call this early twentieth-century transportation surge "the largest public works project ever undertaken by man." It involved the planning of some 40,000 miles of automobile highways. Costing $27 billion (as opposed to the mere millions spent on postbellum railroads), the federally financed, interstate highway system was designed to cross every state in the union and to link or pass near all major metropolitan areas. When completed, the whole system was massive enough to be seen from space. It instantly made the railroads look flimsy, antique, vanishable.

The highways and the multitude of automobiles that came with them could not have existed without the railroads, just as the railroads would not have existed without the steamboats, the canals, and the turnpikes. Curiously—and in a way contrary to what most people regard as the normal historical process—each one of these successive modes

THE DAILY GRAPHIC

AN ILLUSTRATED EVENING NEWSPAPER.

39 & 41 PARK PLACE.

VOL. I—NO. 26.   NEW YORK, WEDNESDAY, APRIL 2, 1873.   FIVE CENTS.

NATIONAL BANKRUPTCY.

THE RIDE TO RUIN.

Extraordinarily generous land grants to railroad companies appear as broad ribbons across the West on the map opposite. Public mistrust in government's dealings with railroads is reflected in the cartoons above.

coexisted with the preceding ones, creating its own traffic, attracting its distinctive quantity of freight and passengers. The meaning of that creative coexistence would have to be understood before modern American transportation could successfully mature.

Railroading in the Gilded Age

The most fervid writers on the romantic subject of American railroads confess (often with strange pride) that the industry had corruption at its heart. Socialistic critics of American capitalism make hay with the excesses of this key industry. Rather than looking at the

self-sacrificing, patriotic Benjamin Judah who pioneered the route of the Central Pacific over the Sierras, such critics concentrate on mustachioed pirates like Thomas Durant.

Deemed smelly enough in his own time to be ejected from the board of financiers (the "Credit Mobilier") that had raised funds for the nation-spanning railroads, Durant and his ejection caused a nationwide uproar. The *New York Sun*'s headlines of September 4, 1872 dared to label him "The King of Frauds." In headlines and columns, the newspaper described "How the Credit Mobilier bought its way through Congress." It spoke of "Colossal Bribery," listing the names of "Congressmen

who have robbed the People and who now support the National Robber." Naming a wondrously precise figure, the *Sun* claimed that Durant and his ring of fellow connivers from New York and Boston had "gobbled" $211,299,328.17 of funds invested by American citizens for the grand purpose of building the nation's railroads.

Corruption did indeed exist. The campaign coffers of Ulysses Grant, among other complaisant politicos, were undeniably stuffed with millions from railroad schemers. And the tragedy of all this was that, when exposure of the corruption became too great for even Wall Street to stomach, the nation plunged into the panic of 1873. The only silver lining in that cloud was that, henceforth, collaboration of government with private corporations for pur-

poses of transportation expansion would be viewed with a certain suspicion; perhaps this was not the best policy. For good or ill, the financial disaster of 1873 drastically slowed railroad development at the very time when the industry's engineering capabilities were being manifested in the Eads Bridge and Hoosac Tunnel.

Yet it did little to criticize the shenanigans of the "railroad barons" who continued to played their titanic games on the national stage. Prime among the barons was New York's Jay Gould who, along with the equally notorious Jim Fisk, defrauded the public of $64 million by watering the stock of their Erie Railroad. Having fled the East with the law behind him, Gould then took his boodle West and, in the key year of 1874, bought control of both the

Union Pacific and the Kansas Pacific. Turning around and selling the latter for a hugely profitable $10 million, he went on to create the most lucrative rail empire in the Southwest.

Respectable Wall Street brokers also became fiercely aggressive players in this, the grandest American contest. Edward Henry Harriman, to name but one of these high-stake players, became obsessed with acquiring the Union Pacific—and finally succeeded in 1898. He went on to grab up as many other western railroads as he could, by means fair and foul. Some saw him as no more harmful than another sort of millionaire who might collect expensive paintings. Antimonopolist President Theodore Roosevelt, however, singled him out as a "malefactor of great wealth." Citing this prime example of baronial corruption, Roosevelt dedicated himself to restricting and reforming the industry at the turn of the century.

So, in the building, the managing, and the manipulating of American railroads, corruption rode along as a kind of industrial devil. From the earliest times, when many western editorialists cried out against the land grants to railroad companies which "gave away" so much of the territory (but which did not, in fact, compensate the companies adequately to clear their debts), the railroad was seen as a kind of financial monster. It exploited immigrant laborers, it wasted wildlife and Native Americans, it cheated passengers at every turn.

Lured by wild graphics and grand openings, as in the posters above, and urged along by travel guides like those at right, railroad passengers in the decades after the Civil War anticipated luxury and fun.

Its very corruptness would destine it to fail as a conveyor for Americans on the move.

Yet Charles Francis Adams, Jr. (grandson of John Quincy Adams and future president of the Union Pacific) spoke out on the other side, in favor of this way of doing business. Railroad construction and management was a risky undertaking that needed doing, and only the most daring would undertake it. "The simple truth," Adams wrote, "was that through its energetic railroad development, the country was producing real wealth as no country ever produced it before. Behind all the artificial inflation which so clearly foreshadowed a catastrophe [the panic of 1873], there was also going on a production that exceeded all experience." Furthermore, if one looks at all the available, interdisciplinary information now available, it's clear that the U.S. government made out fairly well by its investment: For loans advanced, the railroads had paid Uncle Sam back more than $1 billion by 1946. The plains had been settled, the people transported, another transportation medium matured and made ready for superseding.

Rolling Across the Plains

In 1882, a mere dozen years after the opening of transcontinental rail service, nearly a million passengers a year rode the line between Omaha and Sacramento. In these climactic decades of the western railroads, between the 1870s and the 1890s, the constant dangers of western travel and the disinclination of management to do anything much about them were as remarkable as the increasing speed and elegance of the trains themselves.

"Concussions," as head-on collisions were called in those years, occurred frequently, most often because of the rudimentary signal systems between stations on the single-track western lines. Workers, six times more at risk than passengers (modern computations tell us),

Contributing to rail excitement were tales of accidents, Indians, and natural disasters as thrilling as that shown in the Currier and Ives engraving above, entitled "Prairie Fires of the Great West."

Actual travel on western rails involved hardships and boredom, amid amazing scenery. The Currier and Ives engraving above and the newspaper illustration at right show snow-bound passengers coping. Artists poignantly depicted a lonely siding in the Sierra Nevada and "Hotel Life on the Plains," opposite above. They also pictured immigrants' joyless reception at the Union Pacific's Omaha depot, opposite below.

Conductors gave travelers only ten minutes for refreshment at the Great America Tea Co. establishment above. Then they had to scramble aboard while waiters still sought payment. But some found luxury—including the imaginary lady at the right on a travel-route chaise and the group opposite gathered around a parlour car organ.

faced the daily prospect of being crushed between fast-braking cars or mangled by faulty equipment. In the year 1888 alone, 2,070 railroad workers were killed in action, another 20,148 injured.

Before the commencement of this high-speed, high-accident era, when the best locomotives had weighed only thirty five tons and chugged along at about thirty miles per hour, a group of Civil War–trained engineers (George Westinghouse and Eli Janney among them) had sought to make some technological improvements within the industry. Janney's automatic "knuckle" coupler, an ingenious and safe way to connect railway cars, stands out as a leading example of progress.

If the knuckle coupler had existed earlier, the skull of President-elect Franklin Pierce's eight-year-old son Bennie might not have been crushed beneath a folding seat. The accident occurred when the Pierce family's train car was derailed outside of Boston after a link-and-pin coupling snapped. The nation grieved; devout, black-clad Mrs. Pierce concluded that

the president was perhaps now better able to concentrate on his new duties.

Yet even with the new coupler and other improvements on postbellum trains, the United States remained a low-tech, credulous, slow-moving nation, delighted to ride along with whatever rattling conveyances the railroad magnates chose to supply. The well-traveled humorist Artemus Ward joked that locomotives' cow catchers (another American invention) should be placed on the other end of trains; thus high-speed cows approaching from astern might be better fended off.

By the 1880s and 90s, however, Westinghouse's compressed air brake—which could slow the wheels of all cars on a train simultaneously—began to appear in the West, with salubrious results for transcontinental traffic. Other technological improvements of this era (including far better signaling systems, also by Westinghouse) were making for decreased accidents and fewer crushings and manglings of workmen, even as heavier locomotives began to deliver speeds up to fifty and sixty miles per hour. Driven by the wildly competitive philosophy of their owners (which should not be confused with a passion to serve the public), American railroads accelerated their way through the Gilded Age. Our trains became unarguably the best, as well as the most elegant, in the world.

That elegance was found best in cars for tourists and business travelers designed by a former cabinetmaker, George M. Pullman of Chicago. His famous *Pioneer,* the world's first sleeping car, advanced the industry into a totally new mode: Long-distance travel could now be not only comfortable but luxurious. His initial invention of a well-upholstered upper berth, which could be either folded up against the ceiling of the car or lowered for sleeping, was but the beginning of Pullman's pamper-the-rich offerings. By 1867, the inventor-industrialist had gained enough wealth to found his own company, build his own eponymous town for workers, and stake out for himself an empire to rival those of his baronial peers.

The public responded with such enthusiasm to these magnificent "yachts on wheels" that neither Pullman nor his competitors could

CHICAGO TEMPLE
by the CHICAGO RAPID TRANSIT

build them fast enough to keep up with the demand. A sizable percentage of westward passengers were able and willing to pay the $100 for a first-class ticket, which payment did not cover dinners unless an extra $4 per meal was added. Less-affluent travelers had to get meals at stops along the way.

Queen of the Railroad Cities

Like a wheel with hub and many spokes, Chicago and its out-branching railroad lines symbolized the new era. Initially a raw port city at the meeting place of the eastward lakes and canals and the Midwest railroad lines, the city grew all the more prosperous after 1870 when it served to connect East

and West Coast markets. The city became, in the words of Carl Sandburg,

> Hog Butcher for the World
> Tool Maker, Stacker of Wheat,
> Player with the Railroads and the
> Nation's Freight Handler.

Furthermore, it became the gracious host to transcontinental travelers in a variety of lavishly decorated hotels—including the Grand Pacific, whose Romanesque portals bespoke exotic adventure, and the famous Auditorium, designed by Louis Sullivan. For easterners who broke their journey to the west at Chicago, there seemed ample reason to dally there for a few nights of gaslit entertainment.

Chicago's growth at the nineteenth century's end was marked by such structures as the castle-like C&NW Railroad station shown opposite below and the mansion of sleeping car magnate George Pullman, opposite above. The city remained a transportation hub in the next century, with stations for suburban and rapid transit riders, above.

A critical point of Chicago's transportation systems: the intersection of Barge Canal (from the Great Lakes to the Mississippi River) and rail tracks, seen on bridges raised for a freighter, above.

Chicago society, though diamond-studded, was scorned by New York and San Francisco as reflecting the tawdry glitter of railroad corruption. As early as 1849, only a dozen years after the town's founding, a newspaper counted more gambling establishments in Chicago than in Philadelphia; by 1858 visitors could choose among some one hundred houses of prostitution; at the height of the railroad era the city was renowned for crooked politicians and illegal liquor traffic. Nonetheless, having recovered from the great fire of 1871 (which left ninety thousand people homeless, many of them recent immigrants) and the panic of 1873, Chicago presented a sufficiently clean face to the world—being among the first American cities to institute civic reform organizations and voters' leagues—to make its nickname, "Queen of the Railroad Cities," no longer a sneering matter.

This was indeed the era of the railroad city and railroad town. In major transportation centers like Cincinnati and Kansas City, the building of elaborate, even fantastic terminals lent additional excitement to the experience of traveling. In railroad-created towns such as Green River, located in Wyoming Territory "860 miles west of Omaha," the train was the focus of all action. A description of the town read, "Green River City has a population of 500 inhabitants; it has a School House and Church, several Stores, a First-Class Hotel, and a Brewery. All trains stop for meals at the Green River Dining Halls, where beautiful Rocky Mountain Specimens of all kinds can be procured."

To lure travelers to such towns along their systems, the booming railroad companies had unleashed heavy publicity campaigns immediately after the joining of the east-west rails. Turning to Manhattan, they had enlisted the outstanding talents of *Frank Leslie's Illustrated Newspaper*. One of the newspaper's first descriptions of the two thousand-mile westward adventure, written only five days after the driving of the golden spike, ran as follows.

A Journey over the plains was [once] a formidable undertaking, that required great patience and endurance. Now all is changed. The shriek of the locomotive wakes the echoes of the slopes along the Sierras,

104

ATLANTIC CITY
The Playground of the World
TRAVEL BY TRAIN

New York City also prospered as a railroad center, the concourse of its Pennsylvania Station, left, appearing particularly elegant. Holidaying New Yorkers traveled to Atlantic City, whose charms are pictured in the poster above.

U.S. architecture found new ways to express the Age of Railroads: above, a low-lying Atcheson, Topeka, and Santa Fe depot; opposite above, the towered Harrisburg, Pennsylvania, station; opposite below, Walker Evans's photo of the Bethlehem, Pennsylvania, depot.

through the canyons of the Wahsatch and the Black Hills, and his steady puffing is heard as he creeps along the mountain sides. The six months' journey is reduced to less than a week. The prairie schooner has passed away, and is replaced by the railway coach with all its modern comforts.

Through such vivid accounts in *Leslie's Weekly* (whose many volumes can be found in the Library of Congress's stacks and on microfilm), a vicarious traveler of today can journey west with young Leslie himself. He embarked on a five-month excursion in July of 1877 along with various writers, artists, friends, and his wife and dog.

Highlighting the dangers of attacks by Indians, buffalo, bandits, prairie fires, and blizzards, as well as out-of-control locomotives, Leslie and his reporters assured their readers that the cross-continental trip was great fun, wonderfully scenic, and unbelievably comfortable. Those comforts came to include, at least on one especially elegant train called the "Pullman Hotel Express," two libraries, a hairdressing salon, two organs, as well as dinners whose menus never stopped. While watching the moon glow on the Rockies' snowfields, pas-

sengers could enjoy oyster soup, antelope steak, quail, and the finest wines.

A new promotion industry grew up to stimulate a rail-happy public: The engravers Currier & Ives issued romantic prints entitled "Across the Continent" showing the virtues of settling the West with the aid of art and industry; a new breed of travel books described the wonders and thrills of the voyage west. Most popular of these books was the lively *Crofutt's Guide*, which commenced publication in 1869 and, despite some thirty-one competitors, flourished for decades. Yet here, too, the industrial devil of corruption worked his not-so-subtle ways. The editors of *Crofutt's* were bribed by towns along the route to advertise their facilities as possessing special interest, worth an overnight visit, whatever the truth may have been.

Nowhere in *Crofutt's Guide* or its competitors could readers find honest tips about avoiding the many rip-offs that railroads and their agents practiced on passengers—the free passes they gave to influential riders, the rebates to cooperative shippers. The guides, with their tales of dauntless "hayburners" being "sieved" by Indians' arrows, were hardly accurate or clean journalism. But this was all happening in the Gilded Age; such exaggeration and chicanery were expected, blinked at. Why? Perhaps because the whole thing worked, elegantly and entertainingly, if not efficiently or honestly.

The lowest class of riders—after the first-class swells in their Pullmans, after the second-class regular travelers in day coaches, and after the short-haul locals—were the poor and humble third-class passengers. They were typically immigrants, riding in cars designed for neither comfort nor speed, attached to freight trains (and thus subject to endless delays on side tracks as the passenger trains roared through). Delayed, dirty, unventilated, the "immigrant cars" took twice as long to make the passage from Missouri to the West Coast as their swifter sisters. For European immigrants, huddled together on backless wooden benches and enjoying only the most primitive sanitary facilities, the voyage across the plains cost about $40 and was merely a continuation of the miserable passage across the ocean. This was steerage on dry land.

As the era advanced, there was no let-up in the arrogance of the railroad barons. Their attitude was best expressed in the alleged snarl of the New York Central's president, William H. Vanderbilt: "The Public be damned!" His 1882 remark actually applied to complaints made by potential customers who, in the old days, might have flagged down and boarded any one of his Chicago-bound trains at a local stop. But now the New York Central had to compete with the Pennsylvania Railroad's through-trains (called "limited" because stops were restricted to those listed on the schedule); no flag-downs would be tolerated. Vanderbilt, harassed by reporters and suffering from high blood pressure, may not have made precisely that remark about the public, but his intentions were clear: Passengers would have to go along with his new system.

Vanderbilt's New York Central, like the lines of J. J. Hill and E. H. Harriman, set their own rates for passengers and freights, obeyed their own laws. Their property grabs and subsidiary operations such as ferry lines seemed beyond the control of city, state, or nation. In California, antirailroad mobs struck back, wrecking bridges and demanding lower rates. In Pullman, Illinois,

SCIENTIFIC AMERICAN

[Entered at the Post Office of New York, N. Y., as Second Class Matter. Copyrighted, 1890, by Munn & Co.]

A WEEKLY JOURNAL OF PRACTICAL INFORMATION, ART, SCIENCE, MECHANICS, CHEMISTRY, AND MANUFACTURES

Vol. LXIII.—No. 18.
Established 1845.

NEW YORK, NOVEMBER 1, 1890.

$3.00 A YEAR.
Weekly.

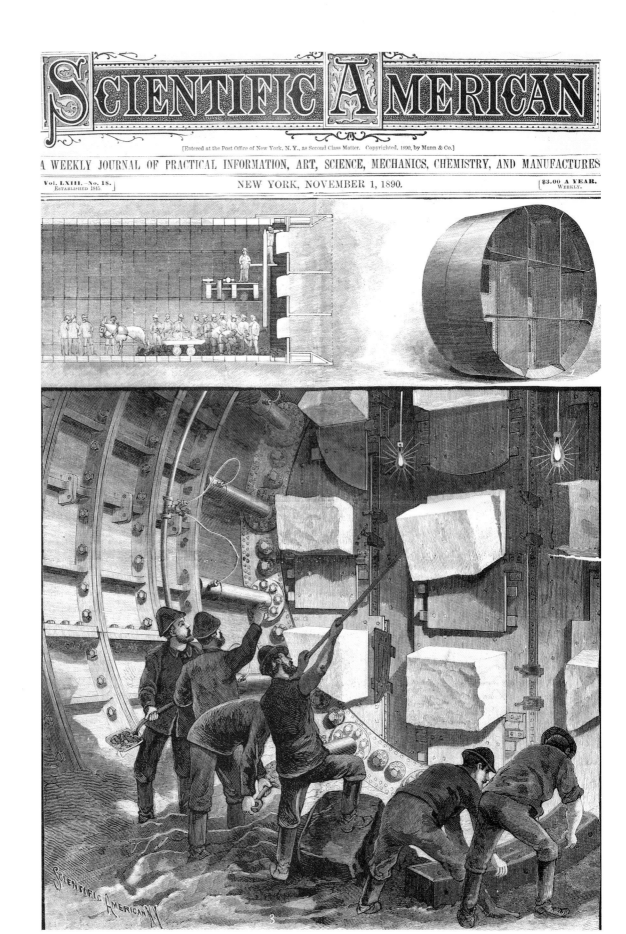

workers led by Eugene V. Debs and the American Railway Union staged a bitter (and unsuccessful) strike against wage reductions.

The Granger movement, in which some 1.5 million western farmers banded together in twenty thousand lodges for social and economic causes, attempted to challenge the railroads in the courts. Throughout the western states, political parties sprang up, reflecting farmers' grievances and pushing for laws to limit freight and passenger rates, abolish passes for the privileged, and create watchdog commissions against the universal corruption.

Predictably, the railroad barons fought back with cannons blazing. Rail lawyers found so many loopholes in the states' "Granger Laws" that most were repealed. Nonetheless, the Grangers had bravely proclaimed the revolutionary concept that railroads might be regulated. Hearing that cry, in 1887 the U.S. Congress created the Interstate Commerce Commission in an attempt to bring railway rates under control. But with the Supreme Court on their side, the barons continued to hold back effective regulation until the administrations of Theodore Roosevelt and subsequent reformers in the early twentieth century. By then, railroads were universally perceived as antidemocratic, requiring the tightest controls for the public good, and generally damnable.

Delights of the Trolleys and Bikes

A year before the famous Pullman strike of 1894—an event that dramatized the railroads' dismal public reputation—two other occurrences demonstrated how dawn-bright was the future of American transportation on other horizons. One was the appearance, on the streets of Springfield, Massachusetts, of an automobile designed and built by the Duryea brothers, a "horseless carriage." The other was the first trip of a trolley car (a species formally termed an "electric interurban railway") in Oregon. To compound this coincidence of car and trolley, it occurred in the very year when Professor Frederick Jackson Turner delivered his famous lecture before the American Historical Association in Chicago, entitled "The Significance of the Frontier in American History."

While describing the America's grand accomplishment of reaching the long-sought western frontier and fulfilling those nationalistic objectives, Turner saluted the railroads in their role of helping to abolish the frontier. He did not, however, peer ahead to predict anything about American mobility and our yen for individual freedom in the postfrontier future—more freedom than the railroads with their high rates and limited schedules could ever allow.

The move in the direction of electrical interurbans had begun in 1888, in Richmond, Virginia, when an electrical wizard named Frank Sprague had electrified a short section of streetcar line. Passengers in Richmond and many other cities small and large had long received service from horse-pulled railcars. Sprague's innovation proved itself at once to be effective, easy and inexpensive to rig up, and swiftly profitable.

The technology of the interurbans seemed within the grasp of any mechanic: A direct current came down from overhead wires via a wand to the car's engine. Rolling along the wire to sustain the electrical contact was a device called a "troller" (as a fisherman *trolls* for his catch; the pronunciation has changed but the concept remains the same). The conductor merely had to supply more or less power to the wheels as speed was needed,

Though America led the world in railroad technology, dreadful accidents occurred—beginning with the 1855 tragedy on the busy Camden & Amboy, above. Accidents also plagued railroad construction. The tunnel workers opposite, however, seem to have everything under control.

"Interurbans," or trolleys, transported many Americans in the early 1900s, prompting the Toonerville Trolley funnies strip, above left, and a host of cartoons, above right.

keeping his eye out for riders. At night, tradition dictated that a passenger would hail the trolley car by means of setting afire a page from his newspaper.

Instantly local lines were built over hill and dale; the clang of trolley bells was heard across the country, particularly in the Midwest. Ohio led other states, developing an amazing network with more than three thousand miles of track. No large town in the state was without service by the time of maximum development, in the late 1920s.

New England, too, sought to take advantage of the new technology, laying down hundreds of miles of track across the countryside. In these well-developed states, however, the lines between towns tended to be extensions of city trolley lines and of those corporations, rather than independent entities. Yet, either way, the sociogeographic fact emerged that no longer was the small-town dweller confined to a limited radius; now mobilized, he or she could travel at will, for shopping, to funerals, or simply for the joy of inexpensive traveling.

Trolley historian Ruth Cavin discovered that trips to excursion spots like beaches and ice-skating ponds tended to be obvious and steady sources of trolley income. For example, because Sandusky, Ohio, has a peninsula thrusting into Lake Erie, with an amusement park and bathing beach at its end, the trolley car conductor on that line found himself able to pass big profits on to his boss. The conductor told Ms. Cavin that in 1916 or thereabouts he worked seventeen and a half hours a day for all of the three-day July Fourth weekend, taking "trippers" to and from the park. "We'd pack 125 people in one car," he said [the cars had seats for fifty or sixty]. They didn't mind the squeeze; they were glad to get aboard."

The totality of the interurbans across America was as impressive as the mode was fun and informal. You could ride from Cleveland to Detroit or from Cincinnati to Toledo

(both trips of about 165 miles) without changing trolley cars. With several changes of cars, the longest possible ride, one enthusiast figured, was from Elkhart Lake, Wisconsin, to Oneonta, New York—1,087 miles. Another interurbanist rode all the way from New York City to Chicago almost entirely in trolleys (using steam-powered railcars for only 187 of the 1,143 miles of track). The trip took him three days, twenty-one hours of actual travel time—he spent nights in hotels along the way—and it cost him less than $20.

Trolleys long held an affectionate place in the American mind, memorialized in song and joke and comic strip. My father and grandfather commuted by trolley, and I grew up feeling that out there over the horizon must be nothing but the delightful landscape portrayed in the "Toonerville Trolley" cartoons. More realistically, these interurbans had the advantage of being environmentally clean, financially affordable by the working class, and tremen-

dously efficient as public transportation. Urban planners confirm that a rail line uses but one-quarter the land needed for a six-lane freeway, while potentially accommodating five times as many people per day. Nonetheless, with the advent of take-you-anywhere automobiles, interurbans almost completely vanished—to the later regret of regional planners.

Besides sheer delight, the major reason for riding the American trolley in its heyday (1890–1930) was that the roads were so terrible, more of a trial than a joy for riders in any type of vehicle. It was the bicyclists who took most vociferous exception to the condition of available roads—and deserve most credit for their political action.

The bicycle—known in classical Egypt but made a potentially long-distance conveyance only when pedals replaced foot propulsion in England in the 1880s—became highly popular throughout Europe when pneumatic tires replaced iron ones at the end of that decade.

As bicyclists became more serious—like the racers outside Washington, D.C., above—and as early automobiles appeared, opposite top, the U.S. public demanded improved roads. The mixed-vehicle street scene in Wilmington, Delaware, opposite below, is a typical turn-of-century traffic jam.

Its popularity spread among both men and women in this country; by 1896, more than a million bikes were being sold annually. Clubs of bicyclists sprang up across the country, clubs that organized themselves into the nationwide League for American Wheelmen.

The major purpose of the League was to promote better main roads and side routes. The League's publications pointed out that, while America's paved city streets were so badly kept as to be difficult to pedal along, the country roads were usually impassable. Gradually certain states began to respond to the call for better roads (a responsibility which, it will be recalled from chapter 1, had originally devolved upon the respective communities). As the nineteenth century ended, a few highways branched out to connect major cities.

But it was the Duryea brothers' curious, self-propelled (by gasoline, not steam) carriage that, having appeared on the Springfield streets in 1893, helped persuade the federal government that an Office of Road Inquiry should be instituted. The purpose of the inquiry was to consider "the best methods of road management throughout the United States." This modern-sounding objective also expressed a reaction to the bad example set by the railroads. Should the nation once again reward the builders of the desired turnpikes with land

grants and fortunes? Or should it take charge itself, constructing and managing the transportation facility for the public good? Or should it simply wait and see, encouraging the states to do something?

Welcome to the Merrie Oldsmobile and the Model T

While legislators dithered about the proper strategies for a national road policy, something unknown in any other culture was happening in America. Inventors and investors, producers and consumers were going ahead to make ground transportation not just a tool for better living but a recognized right of every competent American. By this concurrence of interest in the early 1900s, the mobile character of our civilization was determined for the rest of the century.

Ironically, the technology for this peculiarly American social transformation was supplied by Europeans. Just as we had imported canal building and steam power as well as the bicycle mania from England, so did we import the idea of the commercial, internal combustion engine-powered automobile from Germany. Carl Benz of Mannheim was the genius who—aided by his business-minded wife Berta—was able to translate various mechanical ideas into an effective and popular vehicle (named Mercedes after a favored customer's beguiling daughter). By the late 1890s, the Benz factory was producing nearly six hundred automobiles a year, selling them throughout Europe while facing increasing competition.

In France, a nation blessed with good roads since the imperial reign of Louis XIV, the auto was particularly popular. Paris and other French cities hyped the appeal of cars by staging international races, while also glamorizing the motorcar driver, male or female, as the most fashionable figure of the day. Begoggled chauffeurs began to appear in novels as suggestive sex symbols.

The sporty business of automobile driving grew more slowly in the United States. As late as 1896, cars were still so rare here that the Barnum and Bailey circus displayed one of the Duryea brothers' productions as its main curiosity, with top billing over Jumbo the elephant, the giant, and the fat lady. Electric and steam cars seemed, at first, much easier to operate (requiring no gears) and much safer than the internal combustion engine. Colonel Albert A. Pope, a coach manufacturer and bicycle-manufacturing kingpin in Hartford, Connecticut, who saw some commercial virtue in switching to the manufacture of horseless carriages, decreed that electricity was the way to go. Rejecting an associate's plea to equip the carriages with a gasoline engine, he thundered: "You can't get people to sit over an explosion!"

It was another coach maker, Eli Ransom Olds in Detroit, who came up with an eye-catching little design, the famous Curved Dash runabout, which sold for about $300 and showed America just how much fun an inexpensive gas-powered car could be. Olds's partners had put most of their money on a heavier, more expensive automobile, suspecting that the market lay with the rich and that the rich would consider a runabout too insubstantial. But the partners changed their minds when their factory burned down in 1901 and the only survivor was one of young Olds's little buggies; then the sporty runabout became the focus of all their efforts. "Come along with me, Lucille / In my merrie Oldsmobile!" became the hit tune of the era. By 1904, his company was producing and selling five thousand units a year.

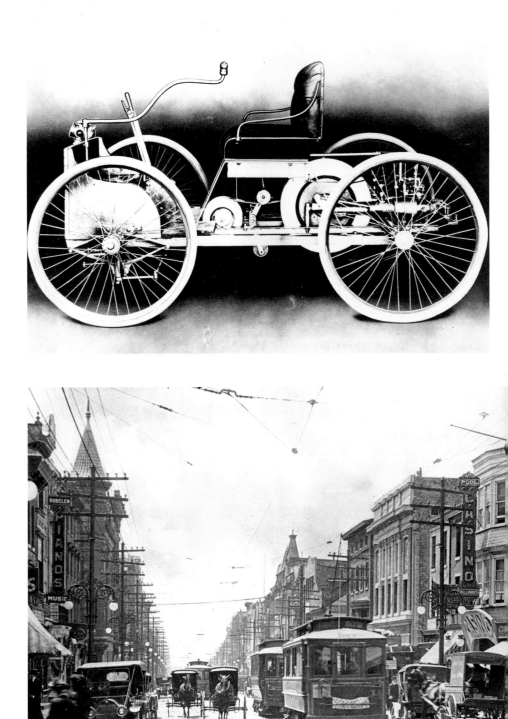

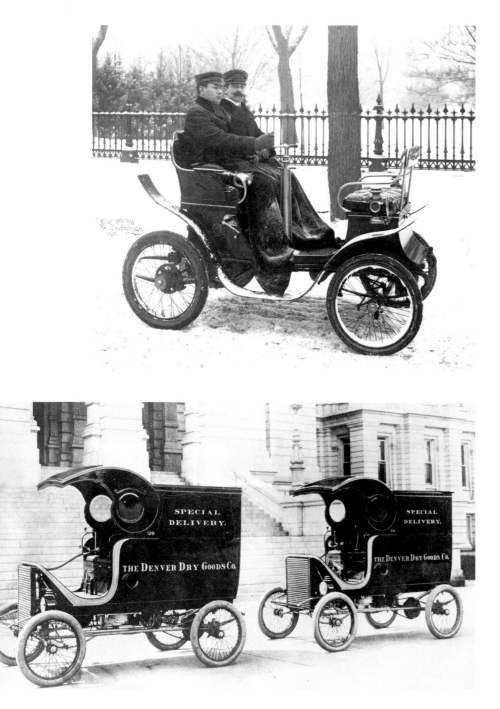

The first autos and trucks, like those above, were steered by tillers rather than wheels and were often wide-open to the elements.

At the same time, Henry Ford, a first-rate mechanic and well-known race-car driver, had succeeded in setting himself up as a budding automobile manufacturer, competing against such solid figures as David D. Buick and James W. Packard. The reason for Ford's emergence as America's and the world's most sensationally productive car-maker lies not only in the cleverness of his manufacturing and selling techniques but also in his understanding of his fellow countrymen: Not custom-made snobs, they were mass consumers.

Ford's egalitarian philosophy was summed up in a remark to a colleague in 1903: "The way to make automobiles is to make one automobile like another automobile, to make them all alike, to make them come from the factory just alike—just like one pin is like another pin when it comes from the pin factory."

Ford believed cars must be mass-produced and low-priced for acceptance by the general public ("a car for the great multitude," as he expressed it). His third principle was that the car had to be simple. The owner—and Ford had in mind someone like himself, the mechanically adept, upcountry kid—should be able to do most of the maintenance and repairs himself. After numerous experiments, he achieved those qualities in 1907 with the Model T, also called the "flivver" or the "Tin Lizzie," the most famous vehicle ever built.

It was powered by a twenty-horsepower, four-cylinder engine that was indeed a marvel of mechanical simplicity, despite a gear system that would defeat many modern drivers. Called the "planetary transmission," this gear setup was operated by foot pedals: If the left pedal was held halfway down with the handbrake on, the car was in neutral; if it was fully depressed, the car was in low; if released, in high. If the driver held that pedal in mid-position and depressed the right one, the car would go into reverse (or, if in forward motion, would be lurchingly slowed down). I remember my mother's oft-told tale of learning how to manipulate these "foolish treads" amid Boston traffic.

With Henry Ford's Model T leading the way, motor vehicle production in the United States rose from 4,000 to 187,000 units annually be-

114

tween 1900 and 1910; registrations in the same period rose from 8,000 to 469,000. Many Americans of the day failed to understand what was happening—the birth not only of a major industry but of a whole complex of integrated industries devoted to the mass production and marketing of a mobile way of life. Census officials, scratching their heads at this unprecedented phenomenon, chose not to recognize auto manufacturing as an industry but, instead, to sweep it under the rug as "Miscellaneous."

Many viewed the ever-rolling new vehicles with concern. Woodrow Wilson, then president of Princeton and studiously aware of certain changes in American society, took a long look at the automobile and concluded it dangerous. He regarded it as "undesirable," if only because a motorcar constituted such an ostentatious display of wealth that it would stimulate socialism by inciting envy of the rich. Instead of being hailed as a hero, Dr. H. Nelson Jackson of Burlington, Vermont, who, in 1903, drove all the way across the country in only sixty-three days, was fined heavily on return home: he had exceeded the speed limit of six miles per hour.

But social critics and old-time legalists who objected to the motorcar were soon left in the dust, as were manufacturers of electric and steam cars. Those short-range or erratic automobiles simply did not appeal to the individual American as much as the predictable products of Ford and other Detroit manufacturers. Numbers tell the tale: the Ford touring car that had cost $850 and sold about six thousand in 1908 fell in cost to $360 by 1916 while sales rose to more than half a million.

Helped by an impressive array of managerial talent, Ford took all possible steps to reduce manufacturing costs while speeding up production. In 1913, he attempted to apply mass-production techniques to the most sensitive part of the engine assembly, the magneto. Succeeding in installing a conveyor belt system for that element, he then experimented with accelerating chassis assembly. Tugging the chassis through his Detroit plant with rope and windlass at a continuous rate, he cut the time of assembly in half (down to little more than six hours). When full assembly-line production was perfected early in 1914, the time

The staid family above prefers the protection of a "Safety Stutz." But the woman at left appears comfortable enough in her open-air Pierce Arrow.

115

AL JOLSON'S TERRIFIC HIT!

HE'D HAVE TO GET UNDER-GET OUT AND GET UNDER

(TO FIX UP HIS AUTOMOBILE)

WORDS BY
GRANT CLARKE &
EDGAR LESLIE

MUSIC BY
MAURICE ABRAHAMS

MAURICE ABRAHAMS MUSIC CO.
1570 BROADWAY
NEW YORK

AL JOLSON

The automobile had made it as a cultural icon by the 1920s. Above is the cover for a car-oriented song sung by Al Jolson; at right, male riders bite their nails as a woman drives.

WHEN WOMAN DRIVES

for chassis assembly was reduced to an hour and a half.

To an astonished world, Ford's full-scale mass-production seemed even more miraculous than the Eads Bridge: Model T's rolled off the assembly line at the rate of one every three minutes, completely identical in engine and chassis. By 1920, every other motor vehicle in the world was a Model T Ford; the competition was all but wiped out. Ford's response to this success was to go for more, and to do that he sought to ensure the loyalty of his trained workers. He advertised for assembly-line laborers at the shocking salary of five dollars for an eight-hour day—about twice the going rate in Detroit at the time.

He also filled the Ford Motor Company's middle and upper ranks with high-caliber employees. Once after World War I Ford arranged to meet a succession of young candidates. After a perfunctory greeting, he asked each young man, "How many steps did you climb on the way up here to my office?" If the candidate had failed to take note and could not answer the question, Ford declined to interview him further; obviously the fellow didn't keep his eyes open.

Nonetheless, Ford's progressive policy of advancing workers and their welfare by profit-sharing (even while spying on them through his "Sociological Department") rattled the cages of conservative businessmen. In 1916 the *Chicago Tribune* called him an "anarchistic enemy of the nation." His radical methods caused one French academic to state in later years that Ford's revolution was a far more deep-cutting and important one than Lenin's.

But that it was not. Benefits of his new industrial system, "the American system," were felt first and foremost among the middle class, not at the lowest depths. Ford's canny sales program (copied by other manufacturers) was financed by dealers well able to obtain loans from their own banks. These carefully selected sales agents bankrolled Ford's supposed revolution while becoming rich themselves—a thoroughly middle-class accomplishment.

As Henry Ford demonstrated in his struggles in the next decades against the United Automobile Workers' union, he was desperately, even childishly, determined to shape the new

116

society of workers, producers, and consumers according to his own small-town precepts. He failed to appreciate that the society that had grown up around Detroit was hardly homogeneous or traditional; by 1930, half of it consisted of either black Americans or immigrants. Finding their cause in unionism rather than in Ford's gallus-snapping preachments, these laborers challenged the company's management with increasing success. After they lost the bloody, notorious "Battle of the Overpass" on May 27, 1937, but won increased public regard, Ford groused that the only thing for him to do was shut his plant down—take his marbles and go home. His wife, with difficulty, talked him out of his pique.

Victory of the Big Three

Ford's dedication to old concepts also nearly lost him his place in the industry. With unshakable devotion, even as other manufacturers surpassed him with better-looking and better-performing cars—including impressive, low-priced models—he stuck with the "Tin Lizzie" through the early decades of the century. Not until 1927 (when Model T number 15,007,003 rolled off the assembly line) did Ford call a halt, introducing the Model A.

During this time of slipping control, Ford lost important shares of the market to General Motors (founded in 1908) which, despite a somewhat roller-coaster-like history, managed to succeed through clever management of a number of complementary lines—Buick, Chevrolet, Oldsmobile—in various price ranges. The GM company's comprehension of how to manage the problem of used cars (manipulating them as stimulants for new sales) and how to design cars with "built-in obsolescence" also helped it to intrude on Ford territory.

Walter Chrysler, like Ford a former farm boy, established yet another ambitious company. Founded in 1921 on the ashes of Maxwell Motors, Chrysler Motors remained profitable through the grim years of the Depression. "The Big Three" American motorcar manufacturers then went on to prove that they had become vital working parts—if not the backbone—of the American economy. In many senses, they were the

Thirties photographer Russell Lee photographed the rear ends of autos outside a new-fangled shopping center of the 1930s, above. They were a far cry from the style of Raymond Loewy's proposed hatchback sedan for the fifties, top.

117

Fragile tires and awful roads remained problems for U.S. drivers as the private auto tempted more to travel. Right, an old touring car makes it through a redwood; below, a bumpy Indiana road challenges motorists. Yet sometimes backroads had charm: opposite above, bridge road to Orr's Island, Maine, and, below a cobblestoned road in Pennsylvania.

industrial heart of America of the mid-twentieth century.

"What of the railroads?" one might ask. Having finally been subjected to rigorous federal and state regulation as a result of their earlier high-handed treatment of the American public, U.S. railroads by 1920 found themselves cursed with declining passenger loads. They had passed their peak both as people carriers and as freight carriers. Motor trucks were beginning to carry heavier and heavier loads for local hauls; soon they would assert their merits for longer hauls.

Roads and Rumble Seats for a New America

The surprising result of the surging production among car and truck manufacturers was that, during the opening years of the twentieth century, the United States had a multitude of individually driven land vehicles long before it had decent roads for them. Although some road building had been carried out in the years since 1900 (when the entire country had only about 150 miles of properly surfaced roads, most in or around cities), newspapers regularly editorialized that the general road conditions were "outrageous."

Recognizing a need for new approaches, wheel enthusiasts and farsighted legislators began to dream of far-stretching, publicly financed roads, even a cross-continental highway. The Road Aid Act of 1916 was passed with that intention: Federal dollars would once more assist construction of the states' roads systems. But to pass the bill was by no means to get the job done.

Meanwhile, the face of America was changing. It was not just a matter of service stations and garages springing up wherever automobile travel existed in reasonable volume. During the 1920s, the commuter by car, the "Sunday driver," and the long-distance tourist with kids in rumble seat became new characters on the social scene. As described by author Sinclair Lewis, small-town America—so isolated and drab at the beginning of the decade—was subjected to the shocks of change and integration at the end of it. The sociologists R.S. and H.M. Lynd, having studied the situation for their 1929 book *Middletown*, found that at all social levels "ownership of an automobile has now reached the point of being an accepted, essential part of normal living."

John Steinbeck painted the picture somewhat more colorfully in his novel *Cannery Row*. He wrote of the moral, physical, and aesthetic effects of the Model T before World War II:

> Two generations of Americans knew more about the Ford coil than the clitoris, about the planetary system of gears than the solar system of stars. With the Model T, part of the concept of private property disappeared. Pliers ceased to be privately owned, and a tire pump belonged to the last man who had picked it up. Most babies of the period were conceived in Model T Fords, and not a few were born in them. The theory of the Anglo-Saxon home became so warped that it never quite recovered.

Yes, Americans acknowledged themselves to be a mobile society. And, as described in previous chapters, this evolution came about not thanks to the automobile alone but to a succession of vehicles as they met the challenge of the land. John B. Rae, author of *The American Automobile*, explained it succinctly: The motorcar "gave an already mobile people

the means to go farther, faster, more freely." But, in a curious and only recently recognized way, automobiles had their limitations (just as did Conestoga wagons, canal boats, and railroads), even while they each enjoyed their own, particular, triumphant times.

Although many attempts to expand America's roadways into a federally supported, transcontinental system failed—especially the "Lincoln Highway," which had started off as a modern version of the ancient National Road and ended up as today's crumbling Route 30—there was a burst of enthusiasm for long, straight roads across the western states. There was also a call for curving parkways in certain, scenic areas of the East ("parkways" being a phrase invented by landscape architect Calvert Vaux). That was particularly true as the booming twenties collapsed in the crash of 1929 and gave way to the public-spirited 1930s when funds were available for building public works. Of these carefully planned, costly roads, the most notable was New York's Taconic Parkway of 1937.

But such gorgeous roadways (influenced, again, by European models) catered primarily to the rich in their Packards and Pierce-Arrows. They had little to do with getting increasing numbers of working-class Americans back and forth on time.

Roadside clutter, a welter of view-blocking billboards, and total confusion of road-building authority, all of which multiplied as America embraced the automobile as its cultural sym-

Cars interacted with other transportation media. Above, in a famous 1935 photo by Dorothea Lange, hitchhikers trudge past a sign for train rides; at right, autos await train arrival at Cochecton, New York, in 1915.

bol, had been only partially brought under control by the Highway Act of 1921 and subsequent interpretations. During the New Deal of the 1930s, the miles of constructed highway in the nation surpassed three million (exclusive of city streets), half of which were characterized as "improved," meaning gravel surface capable of all-weather use. Additionally, the government was taking an increasingly expansive role in coordinating state route numbers and contributing financially to significant road projects.

Nonetheless, it was not until the Commonwealth of Pennsylvania took the lead by establishing the first Turnpike Authority and in building the Pennsylvania Turnpike that Americans began to realize the dream of creating highways to match the capabilities of their automobiles.

Faced with the high cost of roadway construction, Pennsylvanians had fallen back on their own resources—that is, on the well-built but abandoned bed of a railway that had fallen victim to the baronial struggles of the 1870s. Taking advantage of this artifact, the state established a Turnpike Authority, with power to issue bonds and to meet its expenses by collecting tolls.

The 360-mile turnpike, opened in October 1940, proved to be not only a welcome project for the state's unemployed but also a financial success. With curves no greater than 3 percent and designed for speeds of ninety miles per hour, and with neither intersecting roads nor traffic lights, the turnpike seemed an exemplary carrier of high-speed traffic. Other states immediately perceived this as the prototype for the postwar future.

Leader of America's effort to create a national system of highways in the 1950s was none other than General, later President, Dwight D. Eisenhower. "Ike the Builder" he came to be called (along with other affectionate titles), for he had seen the wonder of Germany's *Autobahnen* and was determined to construct an even grander system here. At the national level, Ike retained General Lucius Clay, hero of the Berlin Airlift, to coordinate building the $27 billion program—for which the federal government would pay 90 percent and the states 10 percent.

After World War I, U.S. cities responded to new transportation potentials with plans for moving masses: Above, Boston sets out to build a pioneer subway system; top, New York City designs a rail tunnel under Broadway.

On the local level, such powerful figures as New York City's Robert Moses pushed through legislation for a host of gigantic programs. Many of these highway-building efforts were carried out in the name of "slum clearance" or "urban renewal." Actually, however, neighborhood patterns and social values were mostly ignored by the dictatorial highway builders. Unfortunately the 1956 Interstate Highway laws had overlooked the problem of making proper connections with cities along the way. Builders therefore felt called upon either to bypass them or to blast expressways and throughways into and through the cities' hearts; politicians, for various reasons, agreed with the unleashing of the bulldozers.

It took Americans a generation of such highway brutality to absorb two significant facts: First, that no amount of highway building could decrease traffic jams and congestion (on the contrary, new highway construction merely encouraged the further overcrowding of the reconstructed routes); second, that the problem of intracity transportation had to be resolved by the city, not as part of the interstate highway system, and that the moving of people within the cities of tomorrow was probably best carried out by means other than the automobile.

U.S. Transportation: An Ongoing Evolution

The question of why America remained so long in the grip of the highway builders is closely related to the older question of why America submitted for so many decades to the corrupt rule of the railroad barons. With the highways, the major players—that is, the suppliers of asphalt and concrete, the steel and rubber companies, not to speak of the automobile manufacturers and dealers—gained such a stranglehold on legislators that there was no way highway bills could be turned down or controlled. Alarmed liberals referred to this concatenation of interests, these powerful lobbyists and industrialists, as "The Road Gang." They

seemed to be little more than robber barons, reborn; they also seemed to be the opportunists needed and willing to get a certain job done at a certain time.

This new power group ruled, it must be pointed out, with the glad consent of the governed. While America's cities were slashed and defaced by traffic-producing expressways, while America's countryside was scarred by highways of maximum boredom and environmental destruction, most citizens rejoiced that they could go farther faster. Meanwhile, modern railroads, having attempted a renaissance via streamlined designs, were dismissed (along with trolleys) as no longer relevant. Big cities had simultaneously discovered that subways built in the first half of the century were now so despised as to be stripped by vandals, desecrated by graffiti scribblers.

Some believe that the result of the evolution of American land transportation—over so many decades and by means of so many different modes—has been the ruination of the natural landscape and the forceful manipulation of the popular will. But such doomsayers overlook the character of American society and its resilience. Cities now are attempting to solve their internal transportation problems by means of efficient and popular "metros;" metropolitan areas are binding satellite towns with downtowns by means of light-rail transit systems (as well as hydrofoils and all-weather ferries); metro-liners and limited highway systems are combining to take long-distance travelers where they need to go with decreased impact on the city centers.

Something has been learned from the past: Each of the means of travel that has evolved through history has its helpful place; a sane combination of these, over and against the urgings of new barons and total-solution hucksters, will get us where we want to go in the way we want to go. It appears that the United States is developing today a balanced land transportation system—thanks to the adventures and misadventures of American transportation's distinctive evolution.

In 1928, newly planned
Radburn, New Jersey, above,
epitomized hopes that
American communities could
find ways to live pleasantly
amid the demands of land-
gobbling highways.

Afterword

John Steinbeck, who correctly identified the car as the locus of modern America's most intimate activities, regretted the superhighways of the 1950s. He felt that they made it possible for us to cross the United States without seeing any of the land.

There is much else to be regretted about highways and cars, of course, and it certainly has not been the purpose of this book to hail mobility, gasoline-powered or otherwise, as an unmixed blessing. A generation ago, even as the interstates were being built, the statistics of the consequences of mobility were dire enough to concern many Americans not totally enraptured by auto and highway. At that time, some one and a half million of us were being permanently disabled each year (out of the total four million who were merely bruised in "fender benders"). Yearly fatalities were then more than fifty thousand; now they are double that.

Many other negatives have been heaped upon our seemingly unbreakable contract with the motorcar. These include the "highway hypnosis" that neutralizes our minds each day when we drive thoughtlessly out on our appointed rounds, as well as the manifold problems resulting from air pollution and energy-reserve depletion. Yet—against those seemingly suicidal tendencies and that hopeless destiny—a balanced combination of transportation modes can and will keep us moving as pilgrims across the land, creatively rather than destructively.

When Americans Found Other Ways of Getting About

Perhaps the most convincing historical evidence that Americans can adapt and modify their transportation habits in the face of crisis lies in the decade of the 1940s. Then, with World War II threatening and suddenly upon us, we forsook the ideal of the individual driver to become a nation of carpoolers and bicyclists and train passengers. Transportation was seen as a mass endeavor, a necessary part of civilization's survival, rather than as each person's privileged joyride.

What Henry Ford had given to his fellow Americans—the right to go wherever, whenever they wanted or needed to—once seemed incredible to people in other lands and circumstances. The popularity in the Soviet Union of the film made from Steinbeck's *The Grapes of Wrath* provides one example of this international discrepancy. Communist leaders there had at first boosted the film, believing its grim story of the Depression-bashed Joad family was a telling indictment of U.S. capitalism. But as the picture enjoyed greater and greater popularity, the commissars came to realize that what fascinated the audiences was the depiction of this poor family *with their own car,* driving in pursuit of their own destiny. The commissars therefore canceled further showings; heads rolled.

But this uniquely American right—the right of each family to own a car—can be modified. During World War II, the Joads and their nonfictional counterparts had to "jitney" with others. And many, coping with gas rationing while rediscovering trolleys and other surprisingly pleasant, old ways of getting about, remembered that automobiles had always been chancy things, anyway. In the first decades of the century, those four-wheeled "machines," as they were contemptuously called, seemed likely to disappear as swiftly as they had materialized on the scene. A 1900 issue of the *Louisville Courier Journal* put it this way:

> The present fad in locomotion is the automobile. It is a swell thing, and the swell people must have one. But if it should displace the horse it will only be for a time. The bicycle threatened the thoroughbreds, but where [now] are the bicycles?

So the horse did have its day again, briefly, if only to haul a wagon for the scrap metal in World Wars I and II. Then, in the postwar decades, Americans went car-crazy once more; in the fifteen years between 1955 and 1970, we bought in excess of 100 million private automobiles.

That craziness, continuing today, may be neither terminal nor congenital. Looking back into history, it reminds us of the canal-craziness of the 1830s and 1840s, a time when (as described in chapter 2) the United States committed the folly of spending $188 million on those fragile waterways and going $60 million into debt when there was not the economy to carry such a load. During that memorable canal craze, a state-by-state financial crisis developed, as well as the national panic of 1837, caused by excessive speculation in lands. But the economy had enough resilience to recover, the railroads had begun to chug, bringing with them new passengers, new investors, unimagined economic connections. And to repeat the point made in chapter 3, railroads did not replace either the canals of the East or the wagon trains of the West; they complemented them, creating a very different totality from what had previously existed.

Although the railroads were termed "triumphant" by some, and although they did generate Vanderbilt's public-be-damned attitude (a wipe-out mentality that ultimately did destroy canals and stagecoaches as well as other rail competitors), they soon faced competition from highways and airways. The fact that those modes themselves are now in jeopardy should not make anyone familiar with the history of our overlapping transportation systems faint with despair. A creative tension exists, with government and investors and passengers all pulling in slightly different directions; that's the secret of our ongoing, ever-changing mobility.

We're Mobile—Where Do We Want to Go?

We also do well to recall from the history of American transportation that each new mode of transportation created its own, rather surprising economic justification. Whereas the

Washington, D.C. car owners maneuver desperately to get gas before the enforcement of strict, war-time gas rationing in 1942.

builders of the Lancaster Pike and the Erie Canal and the Central Pacific Railroad and the Model T had hoped that those systems would produce wealth and reward, no market studies existed to assure them of a successful result. On the contrary, many turnpikes in that early era failed; most railroads in the first decade of the steam era were financial calamities; Henry Ford's first company went broke. The wide-spreading market economy that was created by the Erie Canal was a wonderful development that even DeWitt Clinton had not foreseen: His canal delivered goods to an expansive market that had not previously existed. Who imagined that a hundred years later so many Americans could ever be persuaded to buy cars?

The lesson for us is that, although the United States is often seen as driven exclusively by recognizable economic impulses (and thus perhaps best left to the governance of economists), the twists and turns of our society and its evolution have all happened because of people. The eccentric vision of such leaders as Thomas Jefferson and Henry Clay and of such go-for-broke race-car drivers as Henry Ford can create startling, surprising successes. New England financiers tut-tutted at Jefferson's Louisiana Purchase as economically unwise; they were not altogether pleased by Lewis and Clark's report that the development of a rich continent was, suddenly, America's destiny.

This pattern suggests that, for us to be facing a transportation crisis now, at the beginning of the twenty-first century, requires that we ask not one but two questions. Not just, What are the most advisable vehicles? but also, Where do we really want to go, led by whose vision?

We face an ancient challenge—*Quo vadis*, where goest thou? The visions of John Frémont and (in this matter) Brigham Young are no longer applicable. But John Steinbeck's warning, the warning that the straight lines and high-speed potentials of the interstate highways would not let us truly see the American land, seems extremely pertinent. So does a remark made by Native American essayist Vine Deloria. "The trouble with you white settlers," he said, "is that you're too eager to move on. You never develop roots in the land; you never hear its wisdom."

As we moderate our yen to go "farther, faster, more freely" (in the words of auto historian John Rae), we have a new opportunity to investigate the land, explore the variety of neighborhoods, to stop and listen. The national parks and historic sites, many of them now in cities as well as in the wilderness, summon us in a different way than they did in the time of the steamboat bonanza or the railroad extravaganza or the highway spendorama. Rather than going out there to view the curiosities of nature, we can go in there to honor the realities of other Americans and their distinctive communities. We can, as it were, go next door for the first time.

Native Americans—themselves travelers of note—may be giving us, by this advice to get to know our own land and thus ourselves, yet another chance to become Americans more wholly, more peacefully, less wastefully. Let us follow their trail again, like Daniel Boone through the Cumberland Gap.

YELLOWSTONE-PARK

Merrily crowded aboard an old fashioned coach-and-six, travelers to Yellowstone Park at the end of the nineteenth century recall decades of transportation progress.

Bibliography

This bibliography seeks to be more a succinct listing of books and sources that have assisted me—and that thus might be of interest to general readers—than a guide for scholars or librarians. Although *Americans on the Move* is organized chronologically (with many overlaps), a small number of general works were the author's steady companions, including:

Burns, James McGregor. *The Vineyard of Liberty.* New York: Knopf, 1982.

Davidson, Marshall. *Life in America* (2 vols.). Boston: Houghton Mifflin, 1951.

DeVoto, Bernard. *The Course of Empire.* Boston: Houghton Mifflin, 1952.

Dunbar, Seymour. *A History of Travel in America.* New York: Tudor, 1937.

Lavender, David. *The American Heritage History of The Great West.* New York: American Heritage, 1965.

Lynd, Robert S., and Helen M. *Middletown.* New York: Harcourt, Brace, 1925.

———. *Middletown in Transition.* New York: Harcourt, Brace, 1937.

Merk, Frederick. *History of the Westward Movement.* New York: Knopf, 1978.

Morison, Samuel Eliot. *The Oxford History of the American People.* New York: Oxford University Press, 1965.

Schlesinger, Arthur M., Jr. *The Cycles of American History.* Boston: Houghton Mifflin, 1986.

Taylor, George R. *The Transportation Revolution.* White Plains, NY: M.E. Sharpe, 1957.

For chapter 1, which discusses travel during the colonial years and projects the themes of American transportation, I consulted a variety of original and secondary sources, some of whose titles follow:

Bridenbaugh, Carl. *Cities in the Wilderness.* New York, 1938.

Crèvecoeur, St. John de. *Sketches of Eighteenth Century America.* Ed. by Burdin, Gabriel, and Williams. New Haven; 1925.

Filson, John. *The Discovery, Settlement, and Present State of Kentucky.* Wilmington, DE; 1784.

Gallatin, Albert. "Report of the Secretary of the Treasury on the Subject of Public Roads and Canals;" *Duane Pamphlets No. 2.* Philadelphia: Duane, 1807. Reproduction of 1808 edition, Kelley, Augustus M., Publishers, 1968.

Holbrook, Stewart H. *The Old Post Road.* New York: McGraw-Hill, 1962.

Patton, Phil. *Open Road.* New York: Simon & Schuster, 1986.

Shumway, George, Edward Durrell, and Howard C. Frey. *Conestoga Wagon, 1750–1850: Freight Carrier for 100 Years of America's Westward Expansion.* York, PA: Shumway, 1964.

Waitley, Douglas. *Roads of Destiny: The Trails That Shaped a Nation.* New York: Luce, 1970.

For chapter 2, in which the American waterways are explored along with the boats that floated upon them, I found a number of westward volumes that complemented more familiar East-centered sources, namely:

Ambler, Charles H. *A History of Transportation in the Ohio Valley.* Glendale, CA: 1932. Reprint of 1932 edition. Reprint Services Corporation.

Baldwin, Leland, D. *The Keelboat Age on Western Waters.* Pittsburgh; 1941. Reproduction 1980. University of Pittsburgh Press.

Blair, Walter, and F. J. Meine. *Mike Fink, King of Mississippi Keelboatmen.* New York; 1933. Reproduction, 1971. Greenwood Publishing Group, Inc.

Bourne, Russell. *Floating West, The Erie and*

Other American Canals. New York: W.W. Norton, 1992.

Bowles, Samuel. *Across the Continent.* Springfield, MA; 1865. Reproduction, 1991. Reprint Services Corporation.

DeVoto, Bernard (ed.) *The Journals of Lewis and Clark.* Boston: Houghton Mifflin, 1953.

Duke, Donald (ed.) *Water Trails West.* Garden City, NY: Doubleday, 1978.

Flexner, James T. *Steamboats Come True.* New York; 1944.

Fulton, Robert. *A Treatise on the Improvement of Canal Navigation.* London: I. & J. Taylor, 1796.

Goodrich, Carter. *Canals and Economic Development.* Port Washington, NY: Kennicut Press, 1961.

Peterson, William J. *Steamboating on the Upper Mississippi.* Iowa City, IA; 1937.

Strickland, William. *Report on Canals, Railways, Roads, and Other Subjects, Made to the Pennsylvania Society for the Promotion of Internal Improvements.* Philadelphia: H. C. Carey, 1826.

For chapter 3, the exciting era of stagecoaches and early steam railroads, I found valuable both colorful accounts that drew upon the diaries of travelers and more technical studies of transportation development. An abbreviated list follows:

Brown, William H. *The History of the First Locomotives in America.* New York: Appleton, 1874.

Harlow, Alvin F. *Steelways of New England.* New York: Creative Age, 1946.

Nevin, David. *The Expressmen.* New York: Time-Life Books, 1974.

Howard, Robert West. *The Great Iron Trail.* New York: Putnam's, 1962.

Martin, Albro. *Railroads Triumphant: The Growth, Rejection, and Rebirth of a Vital American Force.* New York: Oxford University Press, 1992.

Modelski, Andrew M. *Railroad Maps of North America, the First Hundred Years.* Washington, DC: Library of Congress, 1984.

Moody, Ralph. *Stage Coach West.* New York: Crowell, 1967.

Stewart, George R. *The California Trail.* New York: McGraw-Hill, 1962.

Taylor, Morris F. *First Mail West.* Albuquerque: University of New Mexico Press, 1971.

Walker, Henry Pickering. *The Wagonmasters.* Norman: University of Oklahoma Press, 1966.

Wright, Louis B. *Life on the American Frontier.* New York: Putnam's, 1980.

Winther, Oscar O. *Via Western Express and Stagecoach.* Stanford, CA: Stanford University Press, 1945.

———. *The Transportation Frontier.* New York: Holt, 1964..

For chapter 4, I found myself dealing both with favorable accounts of how America and the world had coped with transportation problems in the past century and with negative descriptions of how our transportation technology had impaired civilization. What follows is a selection from both sides:

Burby, John. *The Great American Motion Sickness.* Boston: Little, Brown, 1971.

Cavin, Ruth. *Trolleys: Riding and Remembering the Electric Interurban Railways.* New York: Hawthorn, 1976.

Flower, Raymond, and Michael Wynn Jones. *100 Years on the Road, A Social History of the Car.* New York: McGraw-Hill, 1981.

Leavitt, Helen. *Superhighway—Superhoax.* Garden City, NY: Doubleday, 1970.

Mowbray, A. Q. *Road to Ruin.* Philadelphia: Lippincott, 1968

Mumford, Lewis. *The Culture of Cities.* New York; 1938.

Nader, Ralph. *Unsafe at Any Speed.* New York: Grossman, 1965.

Rae, John B. *The American Automobile, A Brief History.* Chicago: University of Chicago Press, 1965.

Wheeler, Keith. *The Railroaders.* New York: Time-Life Books, 1973.

White, Lawrence J. *The American Automobile Industry Since 1945.* Cambridge: Harvard University Press, 1945.

Sources

Illustrations for this book were found at various locations within the Library of Congress: Prints and Photographs Division (P&P); Rare Book and Special Collections Division (RBC); Geography and Map Division (G&M); General Collections (GC); Historic American Buildings Survey (HABS/P&P); Specific Subject Index (SSF/P&P); Architecture, Design and Engineering Collections (AD&E/P&P); Popular and Applied Graphic Arts Collection (PAGA/P&P). For those who wish to contact the Library in reference to a certain image in the book, the following guide to locations is provided. Unless otherwise specified, illustrations throughout the book are from P&P. Otherwise, by pages: 5–19, RBC; 25, G&M; 28, GC; 33, G&M; 36–37, RBC; 42, RBC; 55, G&M; 58, RBC; 65, GC; 67, GC; 76, HABS; 103, G&M; 104, RBC, GC.

Library of Congress negative numbers, which may be used to order copies of the visual material in the book, have the following prefixes: LC-USZ62- (b/w negatives); LC-USZC2- or LC-USZC4- (color transparencies). All other numbers indicate the call number of the original materials.

Chapter I: (4) LC-USZ62-3055; (6) LC-USC2-309; (9) LC-USC4-1454; (10) SSF/P&P; (12) LC-USZ62-12627; (13) E 315.F49 (RB); (14 & 15) G 159-B7 (RB); (16) HG 135.R4P6 (RB); (19) LC-USZ62-52626; (20) SSF/P&P; (21) LC-USZ62-36825; (22) LC-USZ62-40673;(24) LC-USZ62-1236; (25) LC-USZ62-40796; (26) FS94.T96 and LC-USZ62-639 (GC); (29) USC4-1304; (32) LC-USZ62-9646; (33) LC-USZ62-51697; (34 & 35) TA 57.591 (RB); (36) LC-USZ62-448; (38) LC-USZ62-10498; (40) HF 1754.G5 (RB).

Chapter II: (44) LC-USZ62-10198, TJ 464.E9; (45) LS-USZ62-1362; (46) LC-USZ62-1342; (47) LC-USZ62-20994; (48) AD&E/P&P, LC-USZ62-39736; (49) LC-USZ62-40065; (50) LC-USZ62-1025; (51) AD&E/P&P; (52) LC-USZ62-10517; (54) LC-USZ62-2676; (55) LC-USZ62-2542; (56) USC4-50; (57) USC2-1724; (58) LC-USZ62-56897; (60) LC-USZ62-24775; (61) LC-USZ62-1079; (62) LC-USZ62-1086; (63) F 593.U58 (GC); (65) F 593.U58 (GC); (66) PAGA/P&P

Chapter III: (69) USC2-3758; (70) LC-USZ62-29713; (72) USW33-36643; (73) USZZ62-21356; (75) LC-USZ62-2508; (76) LC-USZ62-1344; (77) LC-USZ62-104196; (79) LC-USZ62-17897; (80) LC-USZ62-33191; (81) LC-USZ62-12361 and LC-USZ62-20305; (82) LC-USZ62-22877 and LC-USZ62-12361; (85) SSF/P&P; (86) LC-USZ62-12362; (89) LC-USZ62-5398 and LC-USZ62-1312; (93) LC-W33-36635; (95) LC-ZC4-1203.

Chapter IV: (98) LC-USZ62-69756; (99) LC-USZ62-103456; (102) LC-USZ62-35769; (103) LC-USC4-497; (104) LC-USZ62-37840; (105) LC-USZ62-14135 and LC-USZ62-14139 and LC-USZ62-2916; (106) LC-USZ62-1371 and LC-USZ62-1376; (107) LC-USC4-496 and LC-USZ62-1080; (108) LC-D4-12551 and LC-D4-4857; (109) LC-D401-70150; (110) LC-USZ62-84608; (111) LC-USW3-7028D; (112) LC-USZ62-72822; (113) LC-USZ62-54366 and LC-F34-1169-A; (114) LC-USZ62-42031; (115) LC-USZ62-1383; (116) CD-1-A-Fox-1 and CD-1-B-Johnson 383; (117) LC-USZ62-7325 and LC-USZ62-5419; (119) LC-USZ62-45630; (120) LC-USZ62-89764 and LC-USZ62-52091; (121) LC-USZ62-19394 and Poster Collection/P&P; (122) LC-USZ62-2206 and LC-USZ62-77259; (123) AD&E/P&P and F34-38071D; (124) LC-USZ62-58967 and SSF/P&P; (125) SSF/P&P and LC-USZ62-53332; (126) LC-USZ62-55378 and LC-USZ62-24689; (127) LC-USZ62-31602; (131) LC-F34-100563-E.

Index

Adams, Charles Francis, Jr., 97
Adams, Henry, 45, 56
Adams, John Quincy, 34, 48, 51
Adams, John, 48
American Revolution, 55
American Traveler, 66
Arkansas River, 55
Baltimore & Ohio, 51
Barge Canal, 104
Bartleson, John 73
Beckworth, Captain William, 77, 78
Benton, Thomas Hart, 12, 72, 76, 80
Benz, Carl, 112–113
Best Friend of Charleston, 69, 70
bicycle, 111–112
Bidwell, John, 73
Bloomer Cut, 85
Boone, Daniel, 18, 19, 22, 40, 126
Boonesborough, establishment of, 19
Boston & Albany, 50
Bowles, Samuel, 78, 89
Braddock, British general, 22
Bradford, David, 26, 27
Bradley, Abraham, map of 1796, 16
bridge trusses, first scientific analysis of, 31
bridge, suspension, 2–3
Brown, Arthur, 88
Bryant, Gridley, 67–69
Buick, David D., 114
bullwhackers, 79
Butterfield's Overland Stage Line, 82
Calhoun, John, 48
Camden & Amboy tragedy, 109
canal, era, peak of, 49
canals:
    allure of, 45–48
    cost of system, 46
canal boats, 53–61
    description of, 53
canoes, 46
Carbondale and Honesdale Railroad, 69
Carson, Kit, 76
cartoon, "Toonerville Trolley," 110, 111
celebrity wagon, 76
Charleston & Hamburg, 69
Cherokee Indians, 19
Chesapeake & Ohio Canal, 51
Chesapeake Bay, 32
Chinese laborers, 87–88
Chrysler Motors, 117
Civil War, 35, 46, 61

Clark, William, 55
Clay, Henry, 32, 34, 36, 47, 48, 126
Clermont, 65
Clinton, DeWitt, 47–48, 126
Coachman's Guide, 18
Colles, Christopher, 10, 40
Colossus Bridge, 31
Concord coach, 63, 81–82
Conestoga River valley, farmers in, 30
Conestoga wagon, 15, 30, 31, 58, 78
Constitutional Convention, 41
Cooper, Peter, 67–70
    request for railway charter, 69
Credit Mobilier, 94
Crèvecoeur, J. H. de, 3
Crocker, Charles, 87–88
Crofutt's Guide, 106
Cumberland Gap, 13, 18, 19
Cumberland Road, 22, 34, 48
Currier & Ives, 21, 62–63, 97, 98, 106
Davis, Jefferson, 85
Debs, Eugene V., 109
Delaware & Hudson Canal, 66
Deloria, Vine, 126
DeWitt Clinton, 70–71
dugouts, 54
Duke of Bridgewater, 46
Durant, Thomas, 94
Duryea brothers, 109, 112
Eads Bridge, 92, 95, 116
Eads, James Buchanan, 92
Eisenhower, Dwight D., 121
Erie Canal, 22, 44, 49, 50
    completion of, 48–53
    cost of shipping on, 47
    first major American canal, 47
    success of, 47
Evans, Oliver, 36, 38, 39–40, 44–45, 61, 67
ferries, as alternatives to bridges, 32
Fisk, Jim, 95
Fitch, John, 36, 39–44, 45, 65
    misfortune of, 44
Fitzpatrick, Thomas, 7, 76
Forbes, John, 22
Ford, Henry, 114–117, 126
Fort Benton, Montana, 61
Fort Duquesne, 22
Fort Hall, 73
Fort Pitt, *see* Fort Duquesne.
Fort Smith, 60
Fort Snelling, 60

Frank Leslie's Weekly, 76, 86, 104, 106
Franklin, Benjamin, 31, 36, 41
Frazer, Robert, map, 46
Frémont, Jessie, 76–77
Frémont, John C., 64, 65, 76–77, 126
French and Indian Wars, 19
Frey, Howard, 30–31
Frost, Robert, 77
Fulton, Robert, 36, 45, 58, 65
Fulton-Livingston monopoly, breaking of, 61
Fulton-Livingston steamboat, *see* steamboat
Gadsden Purchase, 85
Gallatin, Albert, 7 , 24, 27
General Motors, 117
Gibbons vs. Ogden, 61
gold rush, of California, 12
golden spike, 84–89
Goodrich, Carter, 46–47
Gould, Jay, 95
Grant, Ulysses S., 89, 95
Great American Tea Co. 100
Great Republic, 60
Green River, Wyoming Territory, 104
Hale, Enoch, 31
Hamilton, Alexander, excise tax of 1791, 24, 26
Hamilton, Alexander, federal government in Philadephia, 24
Harriman, Edward Henry, 96, 107
Hartz, Moses, 31
Heck, J.J., 67
Heliopolis, 61
Hill, J. J., 107
Howden, James, 88
Howe, William, 31
interstate highways, 121–122
interurban, electrical, 109–111
Ives, Burl, 50
Jackson, Andrew, 26, 35, 71
    veto of proposed turnpike, 35
Jackson, Dr. H. Nelson, 115
Jackson, William Henry, 74
Janney, Eli, 100
Jefferson, Thomas, 6–7,12, 24, 34, 36, 41, 48, 51, 55, 126
    personal library, 10
Jeffersonians, 34, 35
John Melish's *Travelers' Directory* of 1825, 24
Johnson, A. J. engine, 85
Jolson, Al, 116
Judah, Benjamin, 94
Judah, Theodore D., 85
Kaskaskia River, 34–35
keelboat, 46, 55
Lancaster Pike, 34
    completion of, 27–30
    success of as inspiration, 31
Lange, Dorothea, 120
Latrobe, Benjamin Henry, 40, 50
Lewis and Clark, 46
Lewis, Meriwether, 55

Library of Congess, 7, 36, 45, 65
Library of Congress, 85
Lincoln, Abraham, 54, 84, 87, 92
line barges, 49
Livingston, 58
Louisiana Purchase, 35, 55
Lynd, R.S. and H.M., 119
Madison, James, 48
Main Line Canal, 51–53
map, land grants, 94
Marshall, John, 12–13
Mauch Chunk, 88
Maysville Turnpike, 35
Mexican War of 1845, 12
Mississippi River, 61
    linking with the Pacific Ocean, 66
    population west of, 66
Missouri River, 55
Mitchell, August, map of Texas, Oregon and California, 59
Monroe, James, 34
Mormon emigration, 77
Motor Magazine, 90
muleskinners, 79
Narragansett Bay, 32
National Pike, 27–30, 34
National Pike, *see* National Road.
National Road:
    as a symbol, 34
    bill in support of, 34
    construction of, 6–12
    fate of, 33–35
    high cost of, 34, 35
Neponset River, 60
Nevile, John, 26
New Orleans, 58, 59
New York Central Railroad, 70
Niagara Escarpment, 48
Niagara Falls, **2**
Ohio River, 40
Olds, Eli Ransom, 113
Overland Trail, 65
overlanders, 74
Pacific Railway Act of July 1, 1862, 84
pack train, 79
Packard, James W., 114
packet boats, 49
    see canal boats.
passenger barges, 50
Paterson Iron Company, 60
Pease and Sykes, 31
Pennsylvania Turnpike, 121
Pennsylvania, as "keystone" in arch of national unity, 30
Petty's Island, 43
Pierce Arrow, 115, 120
Pierce, Franklin, 100
pirogues, *see* dugouts.
Platte River, 55
pole-boat, 54
Pony Express, 23, 82–83

Pope, Albert A., 113
population boom, west of the Appalachians during canal-boat era, 55
postal service:
    establishment of, 31
    routes of, 31
    use of the stagecoach, 31
Potomac River, canal along, 35, 48
Potomac Aqueduct at Georgetown, 24
prairie schooner, 72, 75, 78
Proclamation Line of 1763, 15–18
Promontory Point, Utah, 89
Pullman sleeping car, 102–103
Pullman, George, 101, 102
R.E. Lee, 50
Radburn, New Jersey, 123
Rae, John B., 119, 126
railroad:
    ads, 72, 96
    assisting stagecoaches, 65
    barons, 95–96, 102, 107–109
    interest in, 35
    superiority over canals, 66
railway stations, 105–107
Red River, 55, 61
Report on Roads and Canals, 24
Revolution, American, 13, 22, 31, 36, 39, 40, 44
Rivanna River, 6
river crossing, 79
river steamboats, more efficient, 61
River, Ohio, 54
river-craft, as alternatives to bridges, 32
Rocket, 51
Roebling, J. A., 23
Roosevelt, Lydia, 58–59
Roosevelt, Nicholas, 58
Roosevelt, Theodore, 96, 109
Rumsey, James, 40–41
Santa Fe Trail, 65, 77–78
Schuylkill Canal, 53
Schuylkill River, 45
Seneca Chief, 49
Shays' Rebellion, 26
Shenandoah Valley, 22
short-line railway, 70
Shreve, Henry, 36, 61
Shreveport, Louisiana, 61
side-wheeler, as "floating coffin," 60
slavery, 80
Smith, Jedediah, 73
    discover of South Pass, 65
St. Louis Dispatch, 61
St. Louis, as steamboat-prosperous city, 61
stagecoach 81–82
steam engine, and race against stallion, 69
steamboat, 39–44, 54, 55–56
    demonstration of, 41
    Fulton, 40
    romance of, 58
Steinbeck, John, 3, 119, 124, 126

Stephenson, George, 51
Stevens, George, 92
Stevens, John, 48
Stourbridge Lion, 66, 67
Strickland, William, 51
    designs of, 28
Stuart, Gilbert, 7
Studebaker wagon, 21
subways, 121
Suez Canal, 89
Sullivan, Louis, 103
suspension bridge, 23
Tanner, H. S., map of Arkansas, 59
taverns, on sailing vessels, 32–33
Taylor, Zachary, 32
Tocqueville, Alexis de, 35
toll road, sign for, 26
Tom Thumb, 67, 69
Trail of Tears, 71–72
transcontinental railroad, 84–89
travel-route chaise, 100
Trumball, governor of Connecticut, 13
truss bridge, 31
Turner, Frederick Jackson, 109
turnpike, description of, 27
Twain, Mark, 54, 60
Twenty Mule Team Borax, 74
Van Buren, Martin, 32, 33, 48
Vanderbilt, William H., 107
Vaux, Calvert, 120
Virginia, 60
Voight, Henry, 41
wagons, steam-powered, 38–39
Walker, Thomas, 13, 18
War of 1812, 7, 45
Washington, George, 22, 26–27, 48, 50–51
Waterloo Tavern, 18
Webster Canyon, Utah, 86
Webster, Daniel, 69
Wells Fargo & Co., 82–83
Western Emigration Society, 72–74
Westinghouse, George, 100, 102
Whigs, 34
Whipple, Squire, 31
Whisky Rebellion, 24, 27, 30
whisky, as factor in nationwide transportation mania, 24–27
White House, the, 32
White, Canvass, 48
Whitman, Marcus, 72, 75
Whitman, Narcissa, 72, 75
Whitman, Walt, 3
Whitney, Asa, 72
Wilderness Road, 19, 22
Wilson, Woodrow, 115
Winthrop, governor of Massachusetts Bay Colony, 13
Wirt, William, 12
Young, Brigham, 77, 126